(RE)DEFINING THE GOAL

(Re)Defining the Goal

THE TRUE PATH TO CAREER READINESS IN THE 21ST CENTURY

Kevin J. Fleming, Ph.D.

ISBN: 1532912587
ISBN 13: 9781532912580

ACKNOWLEDGEMENTS

To the love of my life, my wife Tamarin. Your patience for my many educational projects is gargantuan. I cannot put into words how much I appreciate your support, without which this book would not exist. I love you more than words can say.

I want to thank my mother, who took me to the public library each summer as a child. I can trace my love of learning back to those early years.

To my writing coach Teri B. Clark. This book would never have materialized without your expertise, advice, and talent. Thank you for taking this journey with me and helping me to grow and learn in the process.

Over the years, I have been blessed to have met many passionate educators in the field. Special thanks goes to these co-contributors that helped me in refining my message, contributing details and examples, editing each chapter, and shaping the final narrative. They are each scholars and passionate teachers whose communities are very fortunate to have them. Thank you for your collaboration, encouraging spirit, and many contributions to this book:

- Bob Tyra, School Counseling Program Co-coordinator, California State University, San Bernardino (CA)
- Dr. Charles Lee-Johnson, CEO, National Family Life and Education Center (CA)
- Clare Bushore, Early Childhood Educator (CA)
- Delores Dochterman, K-12 school teacher, (retired). Editor (CA)

- John Merris-Coots, California Career Resource Network, California Department of Education (CA)
- Karen Miles, Career Pathways, South Central Coast Regional Consortium (CA)
- Michael Modecki, Marketing & Communication, Texas Woman's University (TX)
- Dr. Nick Weldy, Superintendent, Miami Valley Career Technology Center (OH)
- Rita Jones, Coordinator, California Career Café (CA)
- Samuel Hook, Executive Director for Advancement and Foundation, Spartanburg Community College (SC)
- Dr. Shawn Dilly, Superintendent, Mineral County Schools (WV)
- Dr. Virginia Kelsen, Executive Director, College and Careers, Chaffey Joint Union High School District (CA)

To the men of Sigma Phi Epsilon: Thank you for challenging me to be a better man since 1997.

I am thankful for the support, inspiration and camaraderie of the CTE team at Norco College. I am your biggest raving fan. Keep being awesome!

To the giants upon whose shoulders I stand.

All glory to God through whom all things are possible.

*This book is dedicated to
my beautiful wife Tamarin,
who has had the kindness and decency to
not realize she's way out of my league.*

TABLE OF CONTENTS

ABOUT THE AUTHOR

D r. Fleming is a passionate advocate for ensuring all students align who they are with their future career. He is the Principal Investigator for the National Science Foundation's National Center for Supply Chain Automation. He also supports over 35 Career & Technical Education programs as a Dean of Instruction at Norco College (part of Riverside Community College District in Southern California). Dr. Fleming also serves as the Chief Executive Officer of Telos Educational Services (www.TelosES. com) providing keynote speeches, strategic planning, and animated videos to the international educational community.

Dr. Fleming has teaching and administrative experience within 4-year public, 4-year private, and 2-year institutions. He's a scholar, student, recovering academic elitist, and occasionally a rabble-rouser. His perspective is shaped by professional experiences in student affairs, economic development, fundraising/foundations, academic affairs, professional training, and as college faculty at both the undergraduate and graduate levels. Previously, he analyzed industry trends and workforce needs while providing customized geospatial labor market research for the largest public higher education system in the world: the California Community College system.

A true life-long learner, Dr. Fleming has earned two Bachelors of Arts from Loyola Marymount University; a Master of Arts from The Ohio State University, a MBA from the University of Redlands, a Ph.D. from Claremont Graduate University, and a CTE industry certification in geographical information systems (GIS). He is a proud eagle scout, has completed 5 marathons, and won a spelling bee in the third grade.

INTRODUCTION:

OVER-EDUCATED YET UNDER-EMPLOYED

I n my pursuit of higher education, I have earned two bachelor's degrees, two master's degrees, and a Ph.D. I did all of this because I
believe formal education is important. Part of this belief came from
seeing charts like the one on the next page presenting a correlation between higher degrees and higher income.[1] Every chart I saw during high
school and throughout college showed that the average person with a
university degree earned far more money than the average person without a high school diploma.

In the most recent chart of this kind, we see that someone with a professional degree earns about $92,000 more a year than simply graduat-
ing from high school and $74,000 more a year than completing a 2-year
degree.2 Many of my friends and I wanted more earning potential, so
naturally, we continued our education in pursuit of a four-year degree.

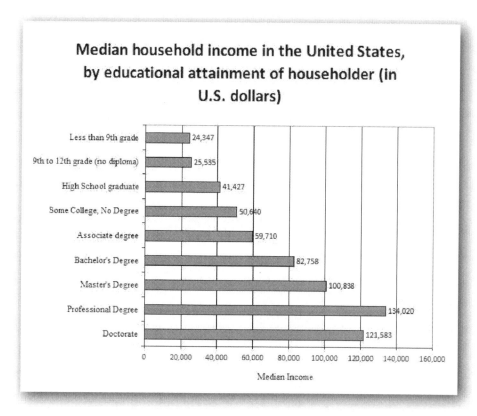

In fact, I figured that if one degree was good, then two must be better. I got one in psychology and one in philosophy. I figured out in my junior year that I didn't want to be a therapist or psychologist. When I graduated, I then found that I could not get a job at the philosophy company! Not knowing what else to do, I went on to get a Masters degree in Educational Policy and Leadership. After all, I knew how to "do" school. Still trying to figure out what to do with my career, I continued on to earn my MBA. Then, in a partial strategy to delay paying off my student loans, I then invested 7 years earning my Ph.D. in Education. By the time I was done, I was over $200,000 in debt and was only making $36,000 a year. I had followed the plan that "promised" to get me the golden ticket to prosperity, yet I found myself in a lot of debt and making far less than I had been led to believe I would be making.

I was well educated, arguably over-educated, but couldn't actually DO anything...at least not anything with in-demand labor market value. I ended up going back to earn an industry certification in Geospatial Information Systems (GIS), and I learned how to make digital maps. I was then able to work for the California Community College system analyzing labor market data on interactive digital maps juxtaposed with map layers of demographics, college location, and other relevant data points. These maps were used to determine labor market supply and demand to adjust college training programs. It was the attainment of specific technical skills which set my career on a new trajectory. This last set of technical skills secured me gainful employment in the labor market. I learned the hard way that the chart of average wages was simply not working for me.

I was not the first, nor have I been the last, to find that a 4-year university education did not prepare me for an initial career. In fact, as you will see throughout this book, educators and parents have taken the idea of higher education to heart, unintentionally leading students towards failure when they thought they were ensuring success.

We know that education is the core to success. However, in order for students to navigate education beyond high school, we must understand the misalignment between our current educational system and our current workforce needs.

University or Bust

This perceived idea that higher earnings are created by having a 4-year degree has fueled a "college for all" philosophy. Educators and parents encourage youth to go to the university – any university – to major in anything – in pursuit of future job security, social mobility, and financial prosperity.[3] This philosophy has increased college enrollment, resulting in sixty-six percent of high school graduates in this country enrolling in higher education right after high school.[4] That's two out of three high school graduates going on to college.

Most people see these numbers and are thrilled. Think of all that potential! How fabulous that so many young people are pursuing a degree. What more could we want?

However, what you won't see advertised is the reality that most drop out and only a quarter of those that enroll will complete a bachelor's degree.[5] Of the quarter that finish, many realize that their degree has not prepared them for the world of work and many have no idea where to start looking to find a career.[6] In fact, many didn't even explore career possibilities because the 4-year degree was going to guarantee them a job making the big bucks.[7] An actual job, however, was never discussed.

There is a big disconnect in how we are preparing our children for the world of work and the realities of the working world. You may be well educated, but not every degree is direct preparation for employment.[8] This misalignment between degrees and job skills causes half of university graduates to be under-employed in what are called gray-collar jobs.[9] They end up taking positions that do not require the education they have received, at a financial cost that is more than they can afford.[10]

The Pot Roast Story

If so many students end up unemployed or underemployed, why are so many still following the same path? It worked for their parents... right? Or did it? Did their parents actually sit down and talk about options, talk about their own paths or what they would have done differently? Chances are, most parents are working in fields that they didn't initially plan on pursuing. This brings us to the story of the pot roast.

A new bride decides to make her first big meal for her husband. She uses her mother's pot roast recipe, making sure to cut off the ends of the roast the way her mother always did. Her husband, having never seen this before, asks her why she cuts off the ends. The bride answers, "That's the way my mom always did it, and her roasts are always perfect." And, indeed, the roast was delicious.

The next time the new husband sees his mother-in-law, he tells her that her daughter made a delicious pot roast using her recipe. He then asks why cutting off the ends makes such a difference.

The mother-in-law shrugs and says, "I don't know. I just make my pot roast the way my mom did, and she always cut off the ends."

The mystery is almost too much for the new husband. He can't wait to spend some time with his grandmother-in-law. When the holidays finally arrive, he gets grandma talking about cooking. He then tells her that his wife makes pot roast using her recipe. However, he wants to know the secret behind cutting off the ends of the roast. The grandma sits back and chuckles. "Well, you see, I don't know why y'all are doing that, but I had a small roasting pan and always cut off the ends so the roast would fit."

Although the reason made sense for grandma, it was no longer relevant for the daughter or granddaughter. Nonetheless, they both blindly cut off the ends of the roast thinking that this little secret made her roast the best-tasting roast around.

This, of course, is just a story that makes its rounds, and you may be saying, "Sure, it is humorous, but it is just a story with no truth." There doesn't seem to be anyone clamoring to take credit for this story, but other real stories have surfaced showing the same phenomenon. In an issue of Reader's Digest in 2001, the following story was published.[11]

"When my friend Dale opens a can, she always turns it upside down to open it from the bottom. One day her young son asked her why. "I don't really know," she said. "My mom always did it that way." She decided to call her mom and ask.

"When we brought the cans up from the cellar, the tops were always dusty," her mother explained. "I couldn't be bothered to clean them, so I turned them upside down and opened the bottom."

As you can see, although humans can be very inventive, we can also get caught up in doing things how they "have always been done." We often apply old solutions to new conditions without considering other options. Well, our cans are probably not stored in the cellar, and we most likely have a pan long enough for an entire roast. Similarly, we often apply old advice regarding education and workforce preparedness without adjusting our advice for the new realities of the 21st century.

Lateral Thinking and Real World Solutions

Let's look at a world social problem to see how this premise works. Many third world countries live in relative darkness. Homes have few, if any windows, and no electricity. Looking at this problem, many would assume that we need to "fix" this problem as we have done in the U.S. That would mean helping to build homes with windows and getting electricity to these remote areas.

The problems with such ideas are endless. These countries often do not have the building materials necessary to build houses like those in the West. Can you imagine the cost of transporting glass for the windows? That alone could make the whole project fail; and what of electricity? This requires not only building electrical plants and all the infrastructure going to the villages but also requires the need for costly fuel for the plants to operate. Once again, it seems that roadblocks run rampant.

If people follow the pattern formed in the West and apply it to these third world countries, solutions seem to be few and far between. This is where out-of-the-box thinking comes in.

Out-of-the-box thinking, or lateral thinking as educators like to call it, is really just a way of looking at an old problem and finding new approaches to solve it. It is looking past the obvious. It is going beyond what has already been tried, especially when what has been tried is failing – like in the idea of creating massive infrastructure where none yet exists. Lateral thinking is creative thinking that rejects the old paradigms and comes up with new ideas.

To understand out of the box thinking, we can look at the Nine Dots Puzzle.[12] To complete this puzzle, you are to connect the dots by drawing four straight lines that pass through each of the nine dots one time without ever lifting your pencil.

At first, the puzzle doesn't seem solvable because people can't use straight lines or don't see beyond the box.

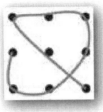

WRONG

Also WRONG

People erroneously assume that the pencil lines must stay within the confines of the square area defined by the dots. If they realize they can go beyond the dots, the puzzle is very easy to solve.

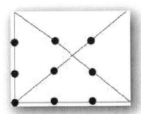

It seems that we can get very stuck in our ways. We don't deviate from our normal route and only see the same options that have always worked. Though this is helpful in many situations, when you have a problem that is simply not getting solved, doing the same things over and over again to fix it is not the answer.

Let's go back to the electricity problem. Rather than looking at the problem from the traditional standpoint, two different solutions have been created that solve the lack of light problem. The first solution creates light indoors during the daytime. Alfredo Moser figured out a way to provide cheap and sustainable lighting to homes with thin roofs via what he called the Moser Lamp.[13] All that was needed was a 1.5 to 2-liter plastic bottle, water, and bleach. The bottle is filled with the water, plus some bleach to prevent mold and algae growth, and fitted into a hole in the roof of a home. The sun shines on the part of the bottle that is outside and refracts the light to the inside of the home. Each bottle acts like a 40 to 60-watt incandescent bulb. No new windows, no power lines, and no expensive fuel.

The second solution is a way to provide light during non-daylight hours and is called a Soccket.[14] A Soccket is a soccer ball that stores energy when used. A child that plays with the soccer ball for 30 minutes will get enough stored energy to power an attachable reading lamp for three hours. Uncharted Play, the makers of Soccket, have since come out with the Pulse jump rope that will give six hours of LED light after 15 minutes of jumping. They hope to figure out other power-generating toys in the future.

New Problems Need New Solutions

This type of lateral thinking must now be applied to education. To meet the challenges of the future, schools cannot be the same as they've been since the 1950's with a few added bells and whistles. Instead, they need to be different to meet the challenges of the new economy. I have sprinkled ideas and best practices throughout this book, especially in Chapters 5-9.

Conventional wisdom, the old way of thinking, suggests that a university degree guarantees a higher salary. But the reality is that with rising education costs, a shifting job market, and the over-saturation of some academic majors in the workforce, this old advice is now a myth for a majority of students.[15] The economy and the world have dramatically changed.

Taking Education Out of the Box

We have gotten stuck because we have been expecting old solutions to solve new problems. We are doing things certain ways because we've been doing them this way for three generations, despite the fact that the *why* behind the reasoning doesn't work anymore. Sadly, the "4-year college education will provide you with a great job" idea is no longer bringing the right solutions to students, yet we just keep pitching it over and over again. This is Albert Einstein's definition of insanity: doing the same thing over and over while expecting a different result.

But it does not have to be this way. We need to realize that not everyone is going to the Ivy League and that this is perfectly acceptable.

Instead, we need to ensure that we are guiding students to careers and not just to the university. It may be hard to accept initially, but in this new economy, a university diploma is no longer the guaranteed path to economic success as it was for our parents and grandparents. Our world has changed.

It's ironic that our dialogue in education now includes the phrase "college and career readiness." Don't all students, without exception, need preparation for work and a career? A nation that touts equal opportunity should provide education in ways that do not sacrifice serious career preparation to instead offer an abundance of liberal arts and humanities courses, falsely assuming that all students will graduate from a university.[16]

Formal education does count, but in our current economy skills count more. For many, a diploma is simply a certification of good attendance. For others, a degree is seen as a marker of grit and resiliency. Indeed, there are many ways to earn a great living and be successful; and in the 21st century, most of these paths require mastering technical skills. Rather than blindly advocating bachelor's degrees as the golden passport to financial abundance, it may be wise to place our advice in context of the labor market and promote with equal tenacity Career and Technical Education in order to ensure the majority of our youth are not unprepared for the transition to the workforce.

The time has come to redefine the goal. It is time to look at education in a new light and change the rules of the game. It is time to try new approaches that solve our educational and economic problems. And, for the record, there are multiple strategies to thinking outside the box, many ways to redefine student success, and multiple solutions to every problem:

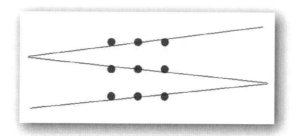

A Few Caveats

This book is organized so that some chapters can be shared individually with a friend or colleague. At the end of the book, there is an appendix just for parents, and another just for students. Thus, some information/sections are intentionally repeated multiple times throughout the book so that each chapter could stand on its own if copied/shared (but of course, buying them their own copy would be the best way to share the information). So note that minor repetition may occur, and it is intentional.

Refined from countless keynote presentations and trainings, this text is intended to build a case for expanding technical skill training and employability skill preparation equal to existing educational efforts. For some readers, this may challenge conventional wisdom that you hold as absolute truth. For others that already share this perspective, my desire is not to preach to the choir but instead to share talking points, examples, and illustrations that help train the militia on the front lines. I hope you adopt and repeat the points presented herein with others to help shape our collective thinking.

Words matter. Terminology matters. Unfortunately, I could not always utilize vocabulary that is ubiquitous across all 50 states. So I ask in advance for your grace. For example, I occasionally utilize *college* and *university* interchangeably throughout the book, when of course there is a distinct and important difference between those terms. Similarly, I chose to use "career and technical education" instead of "career technical education." So, as you read kindly substitute in your mind the terminology that makes the most sense for your local region.

Please also note this is not a comprehensive book on education. It does not holistically explore every facet of high school or of higher education,

Common Core State Standards, graduation requirements, college and career readiness, nor career and technical education. There are many other books on the market that cover these topics far more eloquently than I could. Instead, this book attempts to build the case really for one small sliver of our public education discussion: namely that all students need technical skills and career and technical education (CTE) courses in addition to a strong liberal academic foundation. One without the other is no longer sufficient in the new economy. I believe the data shows that providing students with both, embracing the genius of the 'and', will offer all students the opportunity to be successful in their first few careers.

I have been advised that I also need to state somewhere that this book is an individual effort and is not directly affiliated with any institution or grant project I am currently connected with...so this seems to be a pretty good place to mention this. At the time of this book's publication, I am a Dean at Norco College (part of the Riverside Community College District) and the Principal Investigator for the National Center for Supply Chain Technology Education (funded by the National Science Foundation's Advanced Technological Education program). I also administer a California Careers Pathway Trust grant (funded by the California Department of Education), Carl D. Perkins Funds (funded by the United States Department of Education's Carl D. Perkins Vocational and Technical Education Act), and a Trade Adjustment Assistance Community College Career Training program (funded by the Department of Labor). The opinions and assertions made herein do not represent the attitudes or beliefs of the aforementioned agencies or institutions, nor was this book supported by any grant funds.

Also, some generalizations are made herein, and this may stir up a few healthy debates. I have tried very hard to provide references/end notes wherever possible to the data and primary sources utilized as the equal value of technical education is not just one man's opinion. But some may misperceive some of my comments to be anti-university or anti-liberal arts; they are not. While some of the assertions made in this book may not be mainstream or politically correct, I have tried to be true to both the evidence and the personal experiences known to me. While I do make some generalizations in the book and recognize the potential for controversy, I don't quite think there is a way to avoid that when providing a counter-narrative to the status quo. So, I have simply reported what I have learned. In fact, I hope some of the claims and data presented herein do cause some healthy debate within your local community about the purpose and role of technical education. Even if one disagrees with a particular fact here and there, perhaps we can all agree on the general premise of adequately preparing students for their future careers. I consider any progress, and dialogue, on that front to be worth the investment of time and effort.

1 United States; US Census Bureau; 2014, http://www.statista.com/statistics/233301/median-household-income-in-the-united-states-by-education/
2 http://www.statista.com/statistics/233301/median-household-income-in-the-united-states-by-education/
3 The Conference Board. (2006). *Are they Really ready to Work?: Employers' Perspectives on the Basic Knowledge and Applied Skills of New Entrants to the 21st Century U.S. Workforce.* And: Bosworth, B. (2010). *Certificates Count: An Analysis of Sub-baccalaureate Certificates.* Washington, DC: Complete College America. And: Deil-Amen & DeLuca. (2010). *The Underserved Third: How our Educational Structures Populate an Educational Underclass.* Routledge. And: Gray, K. & Herr, E. (2006). *Other Ways to Win: Creating Alternatives for High School Graduates. Third Edition.* Thousand Oaks: Corwin Press. And: Symonds, W., Schwartz, R., & Ferguson, R. (February 2011). *Pathways to Prosperity: Meeting the Challenge of Preparing Young Americans for the 21st Century.* Report issued by the Pathways to Prosperity Project, Harvard Graduate School of Education.
4 The rate of college enrollment immediately after high school completion increased from 49 percent in 1972 to 67 percent by 1997, but since 2002 has fluctuated between 62 and 69 percent. Source: US Dept of Education, National Center for Education Statistics.
5 Horn & Berger. (2005). *College persistence on the rise? Changes in 5-year degree completion and postsecondary persistence rates between 1994 and 2000.* Washington DC: National Center for Educational Statistics. And: Symonds, W., Schwartz, R., & Ferguson, R. (February 2011). *Pathways to Prosperity: Meeting the Challenge of Preparing Young Americans for the 21st Century.* Report issued by the Pathways to Prosperity Project, Harvard Graduate School of Education, And: Gray, K. & Herr, E. (2006). *Other Ways to Win: Creating Alternatives for High School Graduates. Third Edition.* Thousand Oaks: Corwin Press.
6 Bureau of Labor Statistics. (Winter 2007-08). *What can I do with my Liberal Arts Degree?* Occupational Outlook Quarterly. And: The Workforce Alliance. (2009). *California's Forgotten Middle-Skill Jobs: Meeting the Demands of a 21st Century Economy.* Washington DC.
7 CA Postsecondary Education Commission. And: Deil-Amen & DeLuca. (2010). *The Underserved Third: How our Educational Structures Populate an Educational Underclass.* Routledge.
8 Jacobson, L., et al. (2009). *Pathways to Boosting the Earnings of Low-Income students by Increasing their Educational Attainment,* Gates Foundation/Hudson Institute. And: The Workforce Alliance. (2009). *California's Forgotten Middle-Skill Jobs: Meeting the Demands of a 21st Century Economy.* Washington DC.
9 Industry Workforce Needs Council (www.iwnc.org). And: Gray, K. & Herr, E. (2006). *Other Ways to Win: Creating Alternatives for High School Graduates. Third Edition.* Thousand Oaks: Corwin Press.

10 Greene, K. (Oct 27, 2012). A New Peril for Older Parents: Student Loans They Co-Signed. *The Wall Street Journal.* p.A1&A12. And: Deming, D., Claudia, G., & Lawrence, F. (2012). "The For-Profit Postsecondary School Sector: Nimble Critters or Agile Predators?," *Journal of Economic Perspectives,* American Economic Association, 26(1): 139-164. And: Carnevale, A., Rose, S., & Hanson, A. (2012). *Certificates: Gateway to Gainful Employment and College Degrees.* Center on Education and the Workforce, Georgetown University.

11 *Reader's Digest* (Canadian edition). "Life's Like That." February 2001 (p. 192).

12 Adair, John (2007). *The art of creative thinking how to be innovative and develop great ideas.* London Philadelphia: Kogan Page. p. 127. ISBN 9780749452186.

13 BBC News Magazine. "Alfredo Moser: Bottle light inventor proud to be poor" 13 August 2013. http://www.bbc.com/news/magazine-23536914

14 "Change Agents: Matthews' Soccket lights up lives". USA Today, May 27, 2014. http://www.usatoday.com/story/tech/2014/05/27/change-agents-jessica-matthews-soccket-ball/9013529/

15 Epperson, S. (August 28, 2012). No College Degree Required for these $100,000 jobs. *USA Today.* And: Godofsky, J., Zukin, C., & Van Horn, C. (2011). *Unfulfilled Expectations: Recent College Graduates Struggle in a Troubled Economy.* John J. Heldrich Center for Workforce Development, Rutgers. And: Jacobson, L., et al. (2009). *Pathways to Boosting the Earnings of Low-Income students by Increasing their Educational Attainment,* Gates Foundation/Hudson Institute.

16 Deil-Amen & DeLuca, 2010, The Underserved Third: How our Educational Structures Populate an Educational Underclass. Routledge

CHAPTER 1

ONE SIZE FITS ~~ALL~~ ~~MOST~~ ~~SOME~~ FEW

Four Simple Steps

Can you imagine a world where one size fits all? Everyone would come out of their identical two-story yellow house to get into their identical white 4-door sedan and head off for a Friday night dinner at the same identical mid-scale restaurant. Once inside, they would open the menu to find one main dish available and one drink selection. Afterward, they would head to the movie theater with 10 screens showing the identical movie all starting at the same time. Although this sounds ridiculous, this is the way our current educational model for getting a good job works.

Society has created what author Ken Gray calls the "one way to win" philosophy. The way to win requires that a student follows four simple steps:

1. Graduate from high school
2. Enroll directly into a 4-year university
3. Graduate with ANY 4-year degree
4. Become gainfully employed

We tell students that if they follow these simple steps, they will be successful. We tell them that they will get a job and be happy. We back this up with statistics about how an average person with a college degree earns far more money than the average person without a high school diploma. The rhetoric we use is that college ensures social mobility, future job security, and financial prosperity.

As a result of this "one way to win" belief, over the last three generations we've gone from 13% of the populous stepping into a college classroom to 60% attending some form of higher education.[1] That is two out of three. However, many are not adequately prepared or occupationally focused to succeed. Others are not emotionally or intellectually equipped. Some go to the wrong school. Some will choose the wrong major. Many teens lack "career maturity" and are simply not ready for college right after high school having no idea why they are even there.

What you won't see advertised in any university catalog is the reality that only a quarter of those ever attending any kind of college will finish a bachelor's degree.[2] Even so, at least we can claim that 25% do graduate and are successful...right? Wrong.

Although a small percentage graduate from the university with a 4-year degree in five years or less, having done everything that society has advised them to do, many then find themselves unemployed. It is at this stage that many of them start exploring careers. It is here that many graduates discover that their liberal arts degrees have not prepared them for the world of work.[3] Their degrees in philosophy, sociology, psychology or some other Liberal Arts field have made them well educated, but oftentimes, students find that these degrees were not direct preparation for employment.[4] But let's not pick on the liberal arts; many graduating with a degree in biology or chemistry find the same problem.

Who Is Behind One Size Fits All?

No matter where you look, you will find the message that going to college is the best way to win. The question is: Why is this idea so pervasive?

Parents greatly influence their children to get a college degree. They still believe in the idea that any college degree is better than none at all because that was the case back when they were considering college. In previous times, a degree was seen as a passport to a better life. Most people didn't get a job based on their degree, but the degree showed potential employers that they were intelligent and willing to put in the work. (Incidentally, the popular jargon today for having a strong work ethic in academia and persisting towards graduation is *grit*.)

The problem, however, is that with so many people getting that piece of paper, employers are now looking for more than a degree. They are looking for specific skills, and sadly, are not finding them. In fact, in a white paper written by the U.S. Chamber of Commerce[5], employers discuss the gap between what students are being taught and what they need to know to start at even an entry-level job.[6]

But parental advice rooted in their personal experience is not the only problem. Students are hearing the same thing from educators in their school. They learn quickly that preparing for college is the most important thing they can do in high school.

I have a friend who was a school counselor for years. He and his wife are big career & technical education (CTE) advocates and wanted to enroll their daughter in some CTE classes in high school. Her counselor informed her that the college prep classes were the default curriculum for the district. Not to be deterred, these parents pushed a bit to find out what she could take anyway, and the response was, "She doesn't need those classes. She's on the college track." They ended up making their own arrangements to make sure she had CTE as part of her schedule, but only after an aggressive amount of proactive involvement.

The truth is that educational institutions have policies and practices in place that encourage students to pursue the 4-year university over any other path. For instance, schools give weighted grades to classes that are college prep, such as advanced placement (AP) or Honors classes. Students know, even if not told so, that weighted classes are more important. Additionally, juniors and seniors are inundated with college fairs, classes on filling out the Free Application for Federal Student Aid (FAFSA) and finding scholarships, and even are given excused absences to visit college campuses. Very few programs exist for those looking to something other than a white collar job.

We can't blame educational institutions for pushing this path because they are often judged by the number of students they send on to 4-year institutions. In fact, U.S. News & World Report creates a list of top high schools in the nation each year. Their formula for determining that status of schools is based on testing and college readiness. U.S. News & World Report does not look at career readiness or student employment ratios or technical training at all.[7] Schools are only high ranking if their kids are college ready, so the "one way to win" philosophy just keeps being perpetuated.

The federal and state governments are also involved in continuing the myth through the use of mandated testing. These tests focus solely on skills needed to attend college. There are no mandated tests for technology, vocational classes, or employability skills. The message students receive is that tested classes are important. Classes that teach job-related skills are not.

The idea is further perpetuated in the media. Recent articles in the news suggest that the idea of "one way to win" is still going strong in our culture. Consider the following article titles:

- Fifth graders go to Bay College to get a taste of higher education[8]
- Going "Crazy" About College Choices At The Grade School Level[9]
- Why Free Higher Education Can't Wait[10]

A recent article in *The Atlantic* entitled *"Reducing the Fear of Life After College"* sounded promising. Right out of the gate the author helped frame today's reality quite well:

"Though Bachelor's degrees are now needed more than ever, over the last 15 years the average wage for someone holding one has declined by 10 percent, and the net worth of those under 35 has gone down by nearly 70 percent since the early 1980s. Employers are using the Bachelor's degree as a screening device, but neither students nor those hiring them think the degree proves that the person who earned it is ready for the world of work."[11]

But by the end of the article the author somehow still concludes that a liberal education reduces fear in life after college. Even children's games push the idea of college. Recently, while playing the Game of Life with some children, the first decision I had to make was whether to go to college and incur a $100,000 debt or go straight to work. If the answer was yes to college, then my little car would go through the schooling loop. At the end of the loop, I then had to choose a career. If I didn't initially go to college, I was given a non-college job. As you can imagine, the difference in job earnings was substantial. I realize it is only a game, but the idea was subtly conveyed that you can't win the game of life or support a family without getting a 4-year university degree. There were no other options unless you wanted to eke out a living as something that was deemed less worthy by the game developers, like a plumber or mechanic.

Our students hear about the university as the only real choice from the time they are young and playing board games with their families. They hear this message from family, friends, teachers, and the media. Yet this message is often flawed, or incomplete at best. But today's students are no longer winning by heading off to college with no plan in place. The rhetoric they hear simply must change. It is time to teach students how to be good consumers of education, finding a fit between their abilities, skills/knowledge needed, and labor market realities.

The Degree as a Signal

Isaac Morehouse, CEO of Praxis, wrote a great article in early 2016 called, *The Two Great Secrets of Higher Education*.[12] I believe he provides a very unique perspective to the place and value of a university degree in the 21st century. Mr. Morehouse writes that tuition is paid for one reason: to buy a signal. And such a signal can be valuable to employers seeking to weed out individuals form the applicant pool. He asserts that there is a correlation between completing college and being a better worker on average. But there is no causation. "Harvard doesn't make you more likely to succeed. The type of person who gets accepted into Harvard is already more likely to succeed."

He continues, "Almost everyone objects to calling the product universities sell a signal. They claim it's a big bundle of goods. It's a social experience. It's a network. It's knowledge. It is indeed a bundle of these things and many more, but these are all fringe benefits. None of them are the core product being purchased. When you pay to get your oil changed and the waiting room has coffee and magazines it's a nice perk, but it's clearly not the service you are purchasing. If the auto garage didn't have these comforts you might still go, but if they only sold coffee and magazines without oil changes, you wouldn't."

He interestingly observes that the university is the same. "Whatever other activities and benefits students may derive from their experience, none of them are the reason they are paying to be there. They are really paying for the signal. Period.

It's easy to prove this point. List every other element of the higher education bundle: sports, parties, talks with professors, lectures, books, living with other young people, etc. Now ask which of these would be possible if you never paid tuition? All of them. Move to a college town, sit in on classes, join clubs, go to events, read books, and live the college life to your heart's content.

When you take away the credential at the end, it becomes clear how easy it is to get all the other aspects of college for free or very low cost, and often better. This is also evidenced by the fact that everyone is happy when class is cancelled. What other good do people pay for upfront and then cheer when it's not delivered? It's because the classroom lectures and tests are not the good being purchased. They are an additional cost that must be borne in order to get the real product, which is the piece of official paper. The signal."

While there may be some logistical challenges to his assertions to simply sit in on classes, I am reminded of the movie *Good Will Hunting*, which helped to illustrate knowledge and intellect are not contingent upon a university education. But Mr. Morehouse makes a good point: Student pay tuition because, from their perspective, they have to.

"They have to [pay] to get the signal, because without the signal you can't get a decent job or be seen as a decent human being, so the prevailing narrative goes. The signal is the product. Until that is understood, no amount of tweaking or reforming or innovating any of the other parts of the higher education bundle will matter. And it turns out, you don't need the signal college sells after all."

He continues to point out that not every signal will be worth the price that is paid: "Everyone is thrilled to show you charts and graphs and statistics about the correlation between degrees and earnings. None of that matters. It doesn't matter because aggregates are not individuals and because data can never show causation. What happens to the average of some aggregate does not determine what course of action is most beneficial for an individual. The average Ferrari owner earns a lot more than the average Honda owner. No one assumes this means buying a Ferrari is a great way to improve your earning potential."

I love that point! Yet today's society makes the erroneous assumption that a college-to-earning correlation exists. We encourage students to purchase the Ferrari (e.g. the a BA or MA degree), to improve their earning potential. To the individual, the question is not whether college is a good investment for all young people on average. It is. But you are not average; neither is your student. The better questions to ask are, what signal does your student need to portray in the world to secure gainful employment? How does one ensure the time and effort spent in education is well directed?

The Misalignment

You see, this misalignment between degrees and job skills causes half of university graduates to be underemployed in what are called gray-collar jobs. This means that graduates are taking positions that do not require the education they have received. For example, my first job after earning 2 liberal arts degrees was in foreclosure department of a large mortgage lending company. I literally would fall asleep in the file room bored out of my mind. I was overeducated and underemployed.

The college graduates from the classes of 2013 and 2014 provided these alarming figures which reinforce this reality:[13]

- 49% consider themselves to be underemployed
- 41% earn less than $25,000 a year
- 64% are working outside their chosen career

They followed the one-size-fits-all plan because they were promised happiness and prosperity, and yet they are finding themselves unemployed or underemployed and working in a field they didn't choose.

Let's look for a moment at those getting ready to graduate. They believe they are going to earn more than their peers in 2013. They also believe that their education has prepared them well to join the workforce, meaning they believe they will be working in their chosen career. These beliefs are despite the evidence that earlier grads are not finding this to be true. Why? Because they still believe the one-way-to-win philosophy.

Lack of Career Prep

The perceived higher earnings for having a 4-year degree have fueled this "college for all" ethos, which increased the focus on college prep coursework, college enrollment, and the proliferation of sub-baccalaureate programs. According to data from the University of Texas at Austin, more students are taking longer to graduate, if they graduate at all. For many students, this is due to a lack of planning and advising. They get to college and simply have no idea what they are going to do. Because of this, 80% of students change their majors before they graduate. If they change too late, it will delay graduation.[14]

An acquaintance posted this recently on Facebook. It shows the issues with the one size fits all educational idea - the idea that if you get a degree, the career world will come knocking on your door:

> *The son of a colleague recently graduated with a Bachelor of Science in Business Management with a Special Certification in Entrepreneurial Studies and is proficient in Spanish and fluent in Urdu/Hindi. He has been working diligently to identify opportunities in the Chicago area that are a good fit with his preparation and interests.*
>
> *If you or a colleague are working in an organization that might be interested in someone with this profile and would be willing to speak with him, please let me know, and I will pass your information along to this very talented and able young man.*

It is sad that this highly educated young man has graduated and is just now working diligently to identify opportunities that are a good fit. This should have happened years ago. This should have happened before he got a degree in Business Management and learned Hindi. Here is a young man that followed the one way to win philosophy, but the philosophy failed him. Why else would he have acquaintances of his father post about his career needs on their Facebook page months after graduation?

The "college for all" rhetoric is often interpreted as "university for all." This message needs to be significantly broadened to, "a post-high school credential for all."[15] Students at various educational levels have left school without employable skills, which is setting our children up for failure while costing them and taxpayers millions.[16] All this while the labor market is desperate for highly-trained, skilled technicians.[17] So, how do we help students position themselves for high-wage, in-demand jobs?

Forget About the Averages, Focus on Abilities

Let's assume a student, Karen, is trying to decide whether to become a dental hygienist or a sales manager. You know that Karen is really good with her hands, and she has always been interested in science projects and working with people. You also know that she has difficulty speaking in public and misses assignment deadlines, indicating perhaps a lack of interpersonal skills and project management acumen.

In exploring these careers, you and Karen look up the average income for both jobs. You find that the average annual income for a dental hygienist is $71,110,[18] significantly below the $108.540[19] average wage for sales managers. So, at first glance, it looks as if getting a bachelor's degree in management is a no-brainer.

But, to make this decision correctly, you must start by throwing out the averages. No one is perfectly average. Everyone has unique skills, interests, and abilities. Half of dental hygienists make more than the $71,000 average, and half of sales managers make less than $108,000.

In this example, Karen has the skills and ability to become an excellent dental hygienist and can reasonably expect to be near the top of this pay scale at $96,690.[20] However, she may not have it in her to be an excellent manager because she is only average in communication skills and leadership ability, both of which are very important in becoming a top manager. Therefore, she is likely to be at the lower end of the pay scale for managers making only $53,700.[21] So for Karen, looking at projected incomes aligned with her skills is a more realistic comparison.

Now, this is just one example, but the concept is true throughout all industries.[22] The claim that someone will make more money with an increased amount of education is not necessarily inaccurate, it's just incomplete.[23] In fact, the income for the top individuals in a wide variety of skilled jobs that require an industry credential or 2-year degree is far higher than the average income for many occupations that require a 4-year degree.[24]

And that's not to say that Karen won't go back to school and eventually earn her degree while being a successful dental hygienist. Of course she could. We must emphasize that there are multiple pathways to career success. The secret is to align your student's initial career choice with their skills and abilities. This book will help teach you how to do just that.

Nationally, Associate Degree earners range between $27,000-$72,000, while Bachelor's recipients earn between $35,000 - $100,000. But this data only accounts for the 25th to the 75th percentile of adult workers.[25] This means 25% of Associate Degree holders earn more than $72,000 annually, and 25% of Bachelor's degree holders earn less than $35,000 per year!

Unlike two generations ago, having hands-on skills and perfecting what you're good at can be as valuable (sometimes more valuable) in today's economy than getting a degree in 'something' simply to get one. In fact, a 2013 Gallup-Lumina Poll report on Higher Education found that when hiring, business leaders say candidates' knowledge and applied skills in a specific field are more important factors than where the candidate went to school or their college major.[26]

The time has come to redefine the goal for our children. Is the goal merely high school graduation? Is it getting into any college? Is the goal simply graduation from the university with any degree? Is it high-wage, high-skill employment in today's economy? Or is the ultimate goal a well-paying career where they are fulfilled? If it is the later, a 4-year university degree may or may not be the best/initial option in a given student's educational journey.

Other Paths

A trusted colleague recently shared his story with me:

> *My first job after graduating with a Bachelor's in sociology was working at an Air Force warehouse with no air conditioning in Belton, Missouri. After a summer of 100+ degree heat and 90% humidity, I moved to San Francisco where the only full-time job I could get was as a security guard in a bank headquarters. I worked the graveyard shift with 12 guards, 11 of whom had a minimum of a Bachelor's degree. Two of the 12 had Master's degrees and two others had Doctorate degrees. That is when I started to question the value of a four-year degree with limited CTE skills. I wound up in a school counseling graduate program so that I could help others understand the changes in the economy and what was needed in education.*

The truth is that not everyone needs to go to a four-year university, and as parents and educators, we need to understand this fact and be prepared to consider other options. We need to ensure we're guiding students to careers and not just to college. In this new economy, a university diploma is no longer the guaranteed path to economic success as it was for our grandparents. Our world has changed. The one-way-to-win philosophy is no longer the only way to win. One size does not fit all. As the chapter title suggests, one size only fits a few. This truth may be hard to swallow, and many will resist it, but it is the new truth which must be discussed and understood.

Some will argue that other paths are available to students and even touted by professionals. Let's look at the most popular one: sports. Consider a young athlete who is a great football player but not a terribly great scholar. What does the student hear when entering the guidance office or after-school practices with their club team? "Play hard and play well. Colleges will then accept you on scholarship. Then you can make it to the NFL."

Here are the realities: A new set of statistics has recently been released showing that 6.5% of high school football players get to play NCAA football. Of that 6.5%, only 1.5% play in the NFL and only play for an average of three years. That means that less than a tenth of one percent of high school football players may spend three years in the NFL.[27] The other 99.9% need a real plan for a lasting career to support themselves and their families in the future. Even many of the one-tenth of one percent who do go to the NFL are unlikely to make enough money to support themselves for their remaining years.

We need to stop trying to convince high school athletes that they can support themselves with football. They can't. To say anything less is feeding a false hope. We need to convince high school athletes to find a career that fits their abilities because it is not reasonable to expect them to support their families through sports. Although sports can be a great way to learn cooperation as a team and has the potential to help develop life skills that favor fitness and wellness, they rarely provide a path to wealth. We knowingly deceive students if we send them that message -- and we lack integrity, at best, if we do so.

So, if it isn't always a 4-year education and it isn't sports, what do we tell students? We need to let them know that there are many paths to success. We need to help them define what success means to them, and we can then help them find an individual path that leads to that success.

This isn't as easy as giving everyone the same plan. It will take work and thought and ingenuity. But in the end it will produce happy, successful adults who were able to navigate their education in such a way as to find a career at the end of the path.

The "one way to win" path of a 4 year university education immediately after high school is a legitimate path. But it isn't the only path. What would these additional paths look like? Here are just a few.

1. Career and Technical Education (CTE)
2. Bachelor's Degree
3. Bachelor's Degree in Technology
4. 2-year Associates Degree
5. 1-year technical certificates
6. Regional Occupation Program (ROP)
7. Military Service
8. Online Education
9. A year studying abroad
10. A prep/gap year

11. Private Career Schools and Colleges
12. Full-time Employment
13. Formal Apprenticeships/Internships
14. Religious Missionary Service
15. Peace Corps or other International Volunteer Program
16. Americorps or other National Service Program
17. Volunteer Work
18. Adult Schools

The world has changed, and in this new economy, a university degree is no longer the guaranteed path towards financial success as it was for previous generations.[28] And even if a student does earn one, that education alone may not be enough.[29] In today's highly technical knowledge-based economy, having hands-on skills and perfecting what they're good at can be more valuable than getting a degree in 'something' simply to get one.[30] Employers want to know what a prospective employee can do and what they can do well, not just what degree hangs on their wall.[31] Since new and emerging occupations in every industry now require a combination of academic knowledge and technical ability, we need to ensure that we're guiding students towards careers and not just to the university.

What all this data shows is that success in the new economy is as much about acquiring the knowledge, skills and abilities needed for in-demand occupations as it is to be well educated. Since new and emerging occupations in every industry now require a combination of academic knowledge, career awareness and technical ability, we need to ensure that we're guiding students towards careers and not just to the university.

Education is core to our economy. But, in order to guide our educational systems, and maximize a student's earning potential, everyone must understand the misalignment between education and our workforce. In truly understanding what is required to earn a high wage, students can avoid the traps and misconceptions of thinking that the university is the sole option for financial prosperity.

1 The College Board, *Education Pays 2010*, Figure 2.7; U.S. Census Bureau, 2009b, Table A-1.
2 Horn & Berger, 2005, College persistence on the rise? Changes in 5-year degree completion and postsecondary persistence rates between 1994 and 2000. Washington DC: National Center for Educational Statistics

3 Bureau of Labor Statistics. (Winter 2007-08). *What can I do with my Liberal Arts Degree?* Occupational Outlook Quarterly. And: The Workforce Alliance. (2009). *California's Forgotten Middle-Skill Jobs: Meeting the Demands of a 21ˢᵗ Century Economy.* Washington DC.

4 Jacobson, L., et al. (2009). *Pathways to Boosting the Earnings of Low-Income students by Increasing their Educational Attainment,* Gates Foundation/Hudson Institute. And: The Workforce Alliance. (2009). *California's Forgotten Middle-Skill Jobs: Meeting the Demands of a 21ˢᵗ Century Economy.* Washington DC.

5 https://www.uschamberfoundation.org/sites/default/files/media-uploads/021927_Youth_Employment_FIN.pdf

6 2014 survey conducted by Penn Schoen Berland for the Rockefeller Foundation

7 http://www.usnews.com/education/best-high-schools/articles/how-us-news-calculated-the-rankings

8 http://uppermichiganssource.com/news/local/fifth-graders-go-to-bay-college-to-get-a-taste-of-higher-education

9 http://www.bedfordnow.com/news/2015/nov/24/going-crazy-about-college-choices-grade-school-lev/

10 http://www.truth-out.org/opinion/item/33754-why-free-higher-education-can-t-wait

11 Roth, M. (April 12, 2016). Reducing the Fear of Life After College. http://www.theatlantic.com/education/archive/2016/04/reducing-the-fear-of-life-after-college/477732/

12 https://medium.com/life-learning/the-two-great-secrets-of-higher-education-f2b9a32e23e5#.xdv2hatss

13 https://www.insidehighered.com/quicktakes/2015/05/14/survey-49-recent-grads-say-theyre-underemployed

14 http://college.usatoday.com/2015/12/16/breaking-the-4-year-myth-why-students-are-taking-longer-to-graduate/

15 Symonds, W., Schwartz, R., & Ferguson, R. (February 2011). *Pathways to Prosperity: Meeting the Challenge of Preparing Young Americans for the 21st Century.* Report issued by the Pathways to Prosperity Project, Harvard Graduate School of Education.

16 Fleming, K. (April 2012), *The Inland Empire's Neglected Majority: By the Numbers.* Paper presented at California Community College Association for Occupational Educational. Costa Mesa, CA. And: Symonds, W., Schwartz, R., & Ferguson, R. (February 2011). *Pathways to Prosperity: Meeting the Challenge of Preparing Young Americans for the 21st Century.* Report issued by the Pathways to Prosperity Project, Harvard Graduate School of Education. And: The Workforce Alliance. (2009). *California's Forgotten Middle-Skill Jobs: Meeting the Demands of a 21ˢᵗ Century Economy.* Washington DC. And: Scott, J., and Sarkees-Wircenski, M. (2004). *Overview of Career and Technical Education: Third Edition.* Homewood, Illinois: American Technical Publishers, Inc.

17 Carnevale, A., Jayasundera, T., & Hanson, A. (2012). *Career & Technical Education: Five Ways that Pay along the Way to the B.A.* Center on Education and the Workforce, Georgetown University. And: The Workforce Alliance. (2009). *California's Forgotten Middle-Skill Jobs: Meeting the Demands of a 21ˢᵗ Century Economy.* Washington DC. And: Gray, K. & Herr, E. (2006). *Other Ways to Win: Creating Alternatives for High School Graduates. Third Edition.* Thousand Oaks: Corwin Press.

18 http://money.usnews.com/careers/best-jobs/dental-hygienist/salary

19 http://money.usnews.com/careers/best-jobs/sales-manager/salary

20 http://money.usnews.com/careers/best-jobs/dental-hygienist/salary

21 http://money.usnews.com/careers/best-jobs/sales-manager/salary

22 Carnevale, A., Strohl, J., & Melton, M. (2011). *What's It Worth?: The Economic Value of College Majors.* Center on Education and the Workforce, Georgetown University.

23 Epperson, S. (August 28, 2012). No College Degree Required for these $100,000 jobs. *USA Today*. And: Center on Education and the Workforce, *Valuing Certificates*. (2009). Presentation. And: Osberg, L. (2001). Needs and Wants: What is Social Progress and how should it be measured. *The Review of Economic Performance and Social Progress* 2001. Vol. I pp23-41. And: Fiedrich, M. and Jellema, A. (2003). Literacy, Gender and Social Agency: Adventures in Empowerment, *DFID Research Report 53*. And: The Workforce Alliance. (2009). *California's Forgotten Middle-Skill Jobs: Meeting the Demands of a 21st Century Economy*. Washington DC.

24 Carnevale, A., Jayasundera, T., & Hanson, A. (2012). *Career & Technical Education: Five Ways that Pay along the Way to the B.A.* Center on Education and the Workforce, Georgetown University. And: Carnevale, A., Rose, S., & Hanson, A. (2012). *Certificates: Gateway to Gainful Employment and College Degrees*. Center on Education and the Workforce, Georgetown University. And: Epperson, S. (August 28, 2012). No College Degree Required for these $100,000 jobs. *USA Today*. And: Adler, L. (2010). *California Career & Technical Education 2010 Longitudinal Study*, University of California, Riverside; School Improvement Research Group. And: The College Board, *Education Pays 2010*, Figure 1.5; U.S. Census Bureau, 2009. And: Mitchell, D. (2006). *California Regional Occupational Centers and Programs 2006 Longitudinal Study*. University of California, Riverside; School Improvement Research Group. And: Jacobson, L., et al. (2009). *Pathways to Boosting the Earnings of Low-Income students by Increasing their Educational Attainment*, Gates Foundation/Hudson Institute. And: The Workforce Alliance. (2009). *California's Forgotten Middle-Skill Jobs: Meeting the Demands of a 21st Century Economy*. Washington DC. And: Deil-Amen & DeLuca. (2010). *The Underserved Third: How our Educational Structures Populate an Educational Underclass*. Routledge.

25 Source: U.S. Census Bureau, 2012, Table PINC-03; U.S. Census Bureau, 2012a

26 http://www.gallup.com/poll/167546/business-leaders-say-knowledge-trumps-college-pedigree.aspx

27 http://www.recruit757.com/nfl-dreams-collegiate-reality/

28 Jacobson, L., et al. (2009). *Pathways to Boosting the Earnings of Low-Income students by Increasing their Educational Attainment*, Gates Foundation/Hudson Institute. And: Carnevale, A., & Derochers, D. (2003). *Standards for what? The economic roots of K-16 reform*. Princeton, NJ: Educational Testing Service. And: Scott, J., & Sarkees-Wircenski, M. (2004). *Overview of Career and Technical Education: Third Edition*. Homewood, Illinois: American Technical Publishers, Inc.

29 Carnevale, A., Strohl, J., & Melton, M. (2011). *What's It Worth?: The Economic Value of College Majors*. Center on Education and the Workforce, Georgetown University.

30 Davidson, P. (October 17, 2012). Employment Surges for Community College Grads. *USA Today*. And: Epperson, S. (August 28, 2012). No College Degree Required for these $100,000 jobs. *USA Today*. And: Coyle, Daniel (2009). *The Talent Code*. New York: Bantam Books. And: Center on Education and the Workforce, *Valuing Certificates*. (2009). Presentation, as sourced in "ACTE Fact Sheet". And: Jacobson, L., et al. (2009). *Pathways to Boosting the Earnings of Low-Income students by Increasing their Educational Attainment*, Gates Foundation/Hudson Institute.

31 Achieve, Inc. (2004). *Ready or Not: Creating a High School Diploma That Counts*. The American Diploma Project. And: Corporate Voices for Working Families. (2011). Why companies invest in "grow your own" talent development models. And: Carnevale, A., Jayasundera, T., & Hanson, A. (2012). *Career & Technical Education: Five Ways that Pay along the Way to the B.A.* Center on Education and the Workforce, Georgetown University.

CHAPTER 2

100 GO IN BUT HOW MANY COME OUT?

The Fate of 100 Ninth Graders

As discussed, educational institutions focus their efforts towards educating students in preparation for graduating from high school and enrolling directly into a university in pursuit of a degree. In line with this paradigm is that a high school's state and federal measure of success is based on its rate of college bound students. To this end, a majority of a middle and high school's time and resources are focused on producing the greatest number of enrolled university bound students. However, problems have arisen due to changing social and economic forces. And let's not forget the individual. The one-way-to-win idea does not take into consideration an individual student's interests, talents, capabilities, and deficiencies.

The truth is that the one way to win philosophy is no longer working for our students. We tell them to graduate from high school, go to college, graduate, and come out employed. Ta Da! You win. They are, however, not winning.

To see the true picture, let's take a look at California's numbers. There is a popular saying, "As California goes, so goes the nation." This is true in many respects (economically, politically, socially), but it is also true in regards to education. The state of California is a representative case study for the rest of the nation when it comes to measuring our educational progress. After all, the state's public school system is responsible for the education of more than seven million children and young adults in more than 9,000 schools. In higher education, 24% of all the community college students nationwide are enrolled in a California community college – that's one out of four nationally!

So, this chapter is dedicated to a quantitative analysis to examine the statewide reality about California's educational system. We will determine how many of California's students are, 1) actually graduating high school, 2) enrolling directly into college, 3) how many complete a baccalaureate education, and 4) how many receive commensurate employment after receiving their college degree.[1] The percentages and figures that follow could easily be substituted for any state in America, and sadly, little variation would be observed.

Picture the one-way-to-win philosophy as a funnel with 100 ninth students poured into its mouth. What happens to these 100 students? How many actually succeed in regards to education and employment? Make your prediction now and then read on to find out the fate of those that don't win the one-size-fits-all educational model.

High School Graduation

In the one-way-to-win philosophy, the first step is to graduate from high school. From 2001 to 2011 (the most recent data available to track these students through college) in California's fourteen educational regions, 68.7% of all high school students who began as freshman graduated within four years.[2] We can thus calculate then that 31.3% of California's students had not graduated from high school and are not enrolling into any university. That's right – 31 of the 100 never get past step one and do not complete high school. Put another way, the 31.3% dropout rate translates to over 1.66 million students in California over a ten-year period.[3]

These students enter the workforce with whatever knowledge, skills, and abilities they've gained since starting school. Due to insufficient training programs, most students are not very marketable and not very employable, thus they initially enter the employment market with a deficit.

Although the one-way-to-win philosophy is not the only way to win, we do know that education, in some form, is necessary to help students become employable. High school should be the place to obtain these skills, but many schools are failing almost 1/3 of the students in terms of gaining employability skills.

When asked, students report that they did not like school, could not get along with the teachers or peers, felt that they didn't belong, couldn't keep up with the work, and had failing grades. These are things that schools can address to meet the needs of their students. However, other reasons are also present that have nothing to do with the school, but with the life of the student. These reasons include things such as needing to work, losing a family member, medical problems, or becoming a caregiver.

When looking at the graph below,[4] two reasons that strike me as most telling are "I was bored" and "School wasn't relevant to my life." These two reasons, which may very well be related since boredom often rears its ugly head when classes don't feel relevant, account for almost 50% of drop outs, or 15 of the 100 freshmen that enter into high school. Being held back or failing too many classes accounts for another 32% or another 10 students. If schools could help students be successful in something that was relevant to them, even if they did nothing else, it appears that the dropout rate could be dramatically reduced from 31% to only 6%.

The top reasons students drop out of high school

REASON FOR STOPPING SCHOOL	PERCENT OF TOTAL DROPOUTS
I was kicked out or expelled	0.6%
Pushed or pulled out of school	0.6%
Family issues or problems	0.8%
Lost a family member or friend	0.8%
Financial issues and work	1.2%
Teacher and school problems	1.2%
School environment	1.4%
Residential or school instability	2.0%
Mental health issues	2.1%
I was bullied	2.2%
Physical or other medical problems	2.7%
I was a member of a gang	3.5%
I got pregnant/gave birth	10.8%
I got into drugs	11.6%
I was held back	14.2%
No one cared if I attended	17.7%
I had to make money to support my family	19.0%
School wasn't relevant to my life	20.3%
I became a caregiver	25.9%
I was bored	25.9%
I was failing too many classes	27.6%

SOURCE: GradNation.org   TECH INSIDER

Immediately Attending Higher Education

The next step in the one-way-to-win philosophy is to go to college. Therefore, of the 69 graduates left in the funnel, those that are going to "win" should go on to college. However, we know that 42 of them will graduate from high school and immediately enter the workforce.[5] Thirty-one percent didn't graduate and another 42% didn't go on to get any more post-secondary education of any kind right after high school. Thus, we calculate that 73% of students are not prepared for a success- ful career right out of the gate with the current educational philosophy. Moreover, there isn't room in the university for every student if every single one was able/willing to enroll in the university! Essentially, we are setting up ¾ of our students for academic and career failure from the moment they enter the classroom.

With those high school graduates that decide not to attend college, plus the number of dropouts from ninth through twelfth grade, we have a total of 3,123,501 originally enrolled ninth graders in California who will not immediately attend college. Wow!

This may seem shocking considering all the attention given towards pushing ninth through twelfth graders to enroll directly into the university. Borrowing a phrase from author and educator Dr. Dale Parnell, this group of students is what I have come to call the "neglected majority." These students, nearly ¾ of the population of any high school, need and deserve equal alternatives to the "college prep" curriculum. This neglected majority needs an alternative to the pervasive one-way-to-win mindset and paradigm that is so popular among today's middle and high schools.[6]

Completing that Degree

Our leaky funnel now has 27 students left from the original 100. So far, they are "winning" because they have graduated from high school and found themselves enrolled in an institution of higher learning. The problem is that 43% of those enrolled, approximately 10 students from our initial one-hundred, will never graduate from college.[7]

For many students, the university may be the right answer, but the year immediately after high school may not be the right time. Many students are not prepared emotionally or intellectually to succeed. Others have no clue what career they want to pursue and how college can help them get there. In addition, many students stop attending classes for personal, family, medical or other reasons. Many would presume that academic deficiencies would be the only reason for dropping out, but simple life skills, such as organizational skills, time management, study skills, and financial management also contribute to students dropping out of higher education. Interestingly, many consider these important attributes equally valuable in the workforce and call them *employability skills*.

The hardships and challenges many college students face is daunting. As a college dean, I have met many students who were homeless and living in their car; choosing to pay for tuition and books instead of renting a room. I have met single parents struggling to balance fulltime work with fulltime school in order to provide for their families. One alumna recently recounted to me that she had to choose one day a week to go without food because she simply couldn't afford it. There is a myriad of reasons our students completion rate is so low...many are tragic and heartbreaking. It is due to all of these reasons, and more, which contribute to 43% of college students not completing any certificate or degree.

Getting a Job

Our funnel now has 17 students left inside. These 17 students did what they were told. They completed high school, immediately went on to the university, and graduated with a 4-year degree. They now go out into the real world of employment and become successful. Or do they?

Of those 17 college graduates, the harsh reality is that 10 will be unemployed or underemployed. They will acquire a position that does not require the degree they worked so long and hard for. They will find themselves in debt and unable to pay for their college education because they cannot find a job that reflects the fact that they are college-educated.

Many students graduate with a degree in the "-ologies" such as anthropology, psychology, philosophy, sociology and others. These are great degrees for gaining theoretical information and to help develop critical thinking, but do these degrees equate to employment? The truth is they often do not, especially if left standing on their own. If you were to go to the local coffee bar or ask a taxi driver, you will find that many have degrees that are not being utilized. They are well-educated but are pouring coffee and driving us to the airport.

Why does this happen? Well, far too few students start exploring career paths that will take advantage of the education they worked so hard to acquire. It is only after they search for employment that they realize their degree may not have prepared them for entrance into the workforce. The federal Departments of Education and Labor report that there are 57 predicted jobs requiring a four-year degree for every 100 individuals that earns one.[8] Even if a college degree is attained, in today's landscape the formal education alone may often be insufficient.

Since 10 of our 17 college graduates will be underemployed, only 7 out of our initial 100 ninth graders remain who will "win" the one-way-to-win game. Yet the majority of the public educational system is focused on this small minority, virtually ignoring the 93% of students that desperately need an equally viable alternative.

Instead of rating schools on post-secondary educational attainment, we should rate them on employment. The question should be, "If you start with 100 ninth-graders, how many of them are gainfully employed by the time they are 28?" Shouldn't that be the ultimate goal? While every state and county will have specific numbers that vary slightly, the overall trend is true across America today. With the current paradigm, approximately 7 students out of every 100 stay in high school, graduate from high school, immediately enter into post-secondary education, graduate successfully, and secure gainful employment. That is one leaky funnel.

Current circumstances show that we should not simply direct our youth to get a 4-year degree in "something" under the false pretenses and unrealistic expectations that it will lead to success. The obtainment of a 4-year university degree can be valuable in a number of ways, but it is no longer the golden ticket to financial success that it was for prior generations.

———

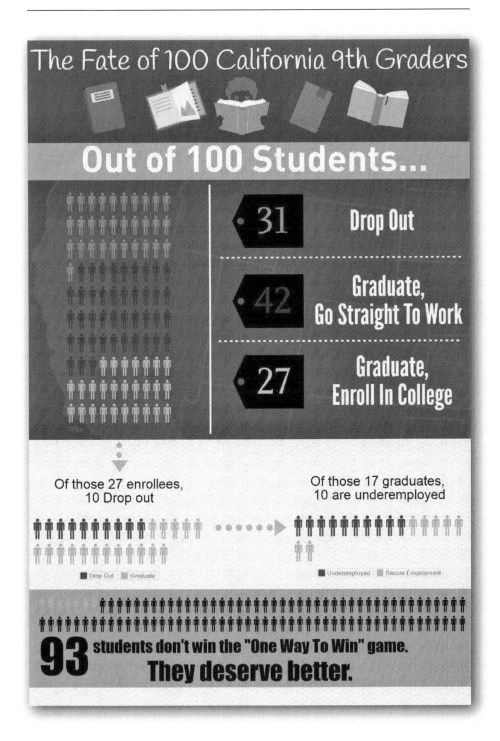

The Fate of 100 California 9th Graders

Out of 100 Students...

31 Drop Out

42 Graduate, Go Straight To Work

27 Graduate, Enroll In College

Of those 27 enrollees,
10 Drop out

Of those 17 graduates,
10 are underemployed

■ Drop Out ■ Graduate

■ Underemployed ■ Secure Employment

93 students don't win the "One Way To Win" game.
They deserve better.

My Friend Mike

My friend Mike is a "success story." He graduated from high school, matriculated into a university, and graduated with a Bachelor's in Film Production. He did exactly what he was told to do, graduating with a university degree – and doing so within 4 years! His story, as far as statistics are concerned, is perfect.

Being an entrepreneur, he didn't look for a job when he graduated but created his own company in music video production. As with most small businesses, he didn't make much money right away and struggled to make ends meet. Student loans, however, don't care that you are struggling with a new business, and once the six-month mark rolled around, his school loan payments began.

He realized that he needed to do something that would bring in enough money to pay his bills while he got his company off the ground, so he went back to school and got a bartending certificate. With that industry credential, he was able to get a part-time job as a bartender. He also went back to school to get his real estate license because the market was booming. He was both a bartender and a real estate agent, all while trying to get his music video production company off the ground.

He soon realized that no one wanted to buy real estate from a 22-year-old with no experience. This caused him to go back to school to get his forklift operator certification. Mike began working at the docks of Los Angeles and Long Beach. Now, as a forklift operator moving goods around the pier while bartending part-time as well, he continued trying to get his business off the ground.

One day he called me on the phone to tell me that he was going back to school. I was a bit shocked. I said, "Go back to school again? You already have a degree and three industry certifications." He said that he had decided to go back to his creative roots and enroll in a very popular for-profit vocational school for fashion design.

This fashion trade school cost him $28,000 for a 10-month program. Here he learned to manage apparel manufacturing processes, and this was going to be his new career. Mike put film and music production behind him, dissolved his film company, and learned a new skill.

Once he graduated from this private vocation school, he became a fabric buyer for the women's clothing store BCBG. Then he got promoted as the raw materials manager for American Apparel, all within two years of graduating. He was finally gainfully employed. I thought he had found his niche until Mike called me one day to tell me that he was not happy. He didn't like what he was doing. He felt there was a glass ceiling, and he had nowhere to go in his field.

Mike wanted to change careers, so he went back to his entrepreneurial roots and began two websites. Despite having no technical experience, he got $50,000 in venture capital, creating even more debt for himself. This was during the MySpace craze, and he was trying to capitalize on the idea of social media. But, neither of his social media ventures, although great ideas, succeeded.

The next time I heard from Mike, he called to ask me if my mom wanted to refinance her mortgage. Then he went on to ask me if I wanted to buy any supplemental life insurance. I asked him what he was up to, and he informed me that he was now a financial planner. He had gone to a program that taught him how to sell life insurance.

I was thinking to myself that he had no business in this profession. He had no experience or background in anything financial. Not to mention that he was a creative guy and financial planning wasn't going to address that at all. But with baby boomers looking to retire in the years to come, doing financial planning seemed like a smart and lucrative field to get into…at least on paper. The local branch he joined crumbled within the year and his stint in financial planning came to an abrupt end.

Mike's professional journey continued on. Next, he went back to his fashion career and designed a casual, plus-size women's clothing line. He tried to sell it to a major clothing retailer, with no success. So he decided to return to his academic roots in film and started working on screenwriting. He applied to screenwriting school at UCLA. He spent over a year writing the required screenplays for their Master's degree program application, only to later discover that the program wasn't necessary to work in the industry.

Mike slowly made his way for years as a freelance photographer, working part time for web designers and as a social media consultant. He is extremely talented, but was unable to secure a stable career…until just recently. As this book was being written, Mike secured a fulltime position as a photographer within a university marketing team out-of-state. His technical skills, combined with his formal education, secured him this position. But it required a geographical relocation, and some humility.

Mike is an academic success story. He did everything "the system" told him to do. He stayed in high school, went to the university, and graduated with a 4-year degree. In the process, he incurred over $150,000 in student loan and business start-up debt and sadly for Mike, he didn't start exploring careers until he was already 22-years-old with a BA in Film Production.

In addition, as is with the case of Mike, the concept of higher education being the guarantee to success is part of the American Dream that many immigrants blindly follow. Mike, the child of immigrants, was told from day one that he must get good grades and go to college. On top of that, he was told to be a doctor, lawyer, or some other professional that was deemed safe and secure. The problem however was that Mike is an artist with a mind for business. The thought of 9-5 workdays bored him to death. Had he known that opportunities existed outside of higher education, he would have most likely pursued photography right out of high school. He excelled in photography. He was the yearbook photographer and photo editor in high school. He was the sole founder of the photography division of the National Art Honors society at his high school. Even as a child, he took photos with his father's camera. Imagine if that passion was identified, nurtured and encouraged earlier? He would have a decade or two of more focused experience, a better established career, and thousands less in student debt. Mike recently told me:

Looking back, photography has always been part of my life since I was a kid. I still have my cameras from different stages of growing up. Unfortunately, I was told that photography (like all art) could never be a career; only a hobby. So my focus was on a paycheck, not on the work. College was supposed to secure a high paying job that would allow me to live and pursue the things I wanted to do. Skilled jobs were never an option. The sad part is, when I have lean times as a freelancer and money is tight, my mother's first suggestion is always to 'go back to school for a higher degree.' I don't even bother explaining why that approach is obsolete and that's what got me into this predicament in the first place. We can't fix the past, but we can influence the future.

We all know someone like Mike. We all have a friend or family member that didn't really utilize their bachelor's degree. We all know someone that struggled to find their fit in the labor market and received little help (if any) from the educational system in securing a meaningful career.

Mike's story reminds me of a line often repeated by my friend and colleague Nick Weldy in Ohio. He often says, "there is no award for being the smartest person in the unemployment line." Gaining academic skills is certainly a laudable and beneficial path for many. But our school systems are mostly established, and funded, according strictly to academic success with little regard to employability potential, labor market realities, emotional maturity, or ever-changing industry needs.

Needless to say, something is profoundly disconnected in American education. We need to (re)define academic success and the purpose for schooling. We also need to (re)define true career preparation. This book is a call to action to collectively shift our concern away from simply one's GPA towards each student's path beyond the ivory tower. It is long overdue to help our students, our family members, and our neighbors, in identifying a career path in line with who they are, what they are good at, and what the world will pay them to do.

Caveat: Education Matters

At this point, I need to provide you with a caveat because I don't want to be perceived incorrectly. I do believe that formal education counts. I am not anti-college, anti-university, nor anti-liberal arts. Quite the contrary. Formal education is extraordinarily valuable. But, what I have learned over the last 16 years analyzing the changing environment of the workforce is that in the 21st century, skills count more. I have earned five degrees and spent more time in school after high school graduation than I did prior. But what enabled me to get out of working poverty was my career & technical education (CTE) certificate in geographical information systems. It was this industry credential that enabled me to gain a tangible skill that employers valued, combined with a strong general education foundation, that enabled me to make progress in my career.

The problem is that our message to students is contrary to the reality of the workplace. We tell students to get a degree, any degree, when in actuality half of students graduating this year cannot find employment based on the general university degree they have secured.

We also tell students that they must get their degree first. I have heard countless well-intentioned parents proclaim that they fear if their student doesn't go directly into a university the fall after high school graduation they may never earn a college degree. Such little faith we have in our youth! The truth is, it may be more feasible to get an industry certification first, start working at a job that will pay $65,000 a year, and then go back to college at a later point (or simultaneously) as their career progresses or changes tracks. Nothing says a student can't come back to school later or in tandem while gaining work experience. Nothing says that you can't get more education along the way while strengthening skills that employers actually value. And truthfully, many students have more career and academic maturity after taking a few years off from school and end up doing better compared to those that aimlessly push forward because their parents told them they had to.

In the 21st century, human resource professionals are trained to no longer look just for diplomas. They are looking for skills. They want to know if a prospective employee can design new software, increase market saturation, or produce tangible results. Yes, they want critical thinkers...but they also want to know if an applicant has the technical skills needed and can hit the ground running. Trust me, and speaking from personal experience, a degree in philosophy may make one a better critical thinker, but it doesn't develop the actual skills needed by today's employers.

Students do need a formal education. They simply all do not need the same education, in the same way, over the same period of time. One's education is best received when it is contextualized into their intentionally selected initial career aspiration. We need to reexamine the one-way-to-win philosophy and change it to many-ways-to-win so that not only 7% of our students see themselves as the winners they truly are.

---

1 Due to variances in statistical data from state, federal, and independent sources, the primary data sources presented here will be taken from those prepared by the California Department of Education (CDE) and the California Postsecondary Education Commission (CPEC). Other primary and secondary sources will be cited if valid and corroborated.

2 Data compiled from California Department of Education – "Statewide Enrollment Reports," and "Enrollment, Graduation, and Dropouts." According to a CDE news release, a new formula was implemented and has served as a baseline in 2011. The new graduate and dropout "…completer rate did not account for students who transferred into or out of schools over four years and overestimated the graduation rate. The new cohort rate takes students mobility into account." CDE New Release, Release: #11-54, August 11, 2011.

3 Compiled from a report from the CDE, the actual number is 1,661,415. To further illustrate: The dropout number translates to 4.4% of California's estimated current population of 38,041,430.

4 http://gradnation.org/sites/default/files/DCTD%20Final%20Full.pdf

5 California Postsecondary Education Commission. College Going Rates Options: College Going Rates to Public Colleges and Universities.

6 Quotes taken from: Dr. Dale Parnell, *The Neglected Majority* (Washington D.C.: Community College Press, 1986). Full credit is extended to Dr. Parnell for the term "The Neglected Majority" – modified with permission.

7 Extrapolated from California Postsecondary Education Commission, Graduation Rates: Graduation Rates for Students Starting College in 2001. Here 2001 freshman enrollment and graduation rates were compiled and extracted from the University of California, California State Universities, accredited non-public 4-year institutions, and state approved institutions. California Community Colleges and other two year institutions were not included

8 Kenneth Carter Gray and Edwin L. Herr, *Other Ways to Win: Creating Alternatives for High School Graduates* (Thousand Oaks, CA: Corwin Press, 2006), cited from the Federal Departments of Education and Labor.

CHAPTER 3

Twenty-first Century High School Education

How We Got Where We Are

We haven't always structured education the way it is now. In fact, our current system is less than 100 years old.

The idea of a public school system was first suggested by Thomas Jefferson around the time of the signing of the Declaration of Independence. He believed that education should be a government function and available to everyone, regardless of their status in society. He was not alone in his thinking. His contemporaries, such as Noah Webster and George Washington, also felt that public education was essential to the growth of our country. However, due to the turbulence of the times, public education didn't really come into its own until decades later.

In the mid-1800s, the Common School Journal was started by Horace Mann. In this journal, Mann took educational issues to the public, arguing that public schooling would be good for everyone. He believed it would unite the country, prevent crime, and eradicate poverty. Due to his herculean efforts, free public education for elementary students became available to all American children by the end of the 19th century.

By 1918, all states had passed laws requiring children to attend elementary school. Initially, states intended for all schooling to be public, but in 1925, the Supreme Court ruled in *Pierce v Society of Sisters*[1] that children did have to attend school, but that the school did not have to be public. Thus began our system of a public education with a choice for private education at a parent's discretion.

High schools, once only for the very wealthy, began their meteoric rise during the 20th century. Dr. Virginia Kelsen reports that high schools came about in response to the great depression, primarily as a way for the states to keep youth out of the workforce when jobs were scarce. Prom, yearbooks, and athletic teams were expanded to draw students in and keep them out of the job market. As a result, high school graduation rates went from a mere 6% to approximately 85% between 1900 and 1996.[2] This was due to the eventual compulsory education laws that required students to attend school through the age of 16.

Since the 1980s, states have been giving high levels of attention to raising academic standards due to a report in April of 1983 called A Nation At Risk, which indicated that our public schools had terribly low achievement, putting our country at risk of remaining globally competitive and providing for her citizenry.[3]

Some of the indicators of risks outlined in this report include:

- Students were not first or second place in 19 academic tests compared to other nations
- 23 million adults were functionally illiterate
- 13% of high school seniors were functionally illiterate
- High school achievement was lower than it was 26 years ago
- SAT scores were down, with verbal scores falling 50 points and math falling 40 points
- 40% of high school seniors could not draw inferences from written material
- Only 20% of high school seniors could write a persuasive essay
- Science achievement scores had been steadily declining since 1969
- Remedial math courses in colleges had increased by 72%

This report also concluded that business and military leaders spent millions to re-educate and train people just so they could begin the training necessary to compete in the workplace. A Nation at Risk called for a host of reforms aimed to right the direction of education in America.

States responded with many different reforms, including higher standards for classes, more frequent testing, increasing teacher credentials and professional development, and more state-mandated curriculum requirements.

My wife's grandmother was an elementary school teacher at the time the report was released and clearly remembers feeling increased pressure as a result. She was even asked to separate out the top math students so that they could proceed independently. Staggered reading programs proliferated and standardized testing increased throughout the 1980s. Overall, however, the report didn't really lead to significant changes. Many of the problems discussed over thirty years ago still remain unaddressed today.

Since A Nation at Risk

Prior to 1980, many programs had been scaled back after the race to space "Sputnik challenge" was over. The report felt this was a key to the problems in education and stated, "Moreover, we have dismantled essential support systems which helped make those gains possible. We have, in effect, been committing an act of unthinking, unilateral educational disarmament."[4]

Although this may have been true in 1983, it is even truer today. Educational budget cuts, along with rigorous standardized testing have narrowed the curriculum choices. From 1987 to 2003, prior to the standardized testing movement known as No Child Left Behind, time allocation for subjects remained about the same with two hours a day going to language arts, one hour to math, and 30 minutes each to social studies and science.[5] Since 2003, however, time allocation has changed tremendously in response to the testing. Schools that were identified as needing improvement were found to increase their language arts time by 47% and their math by 37%. To accommodate this additional time, these schools decreased time allotted to other activities such as social studies, science, art, physical education, recess, and music.[6] Teachers lamented these changes and children resisted.

Such rigorous tests also precluded using a wide variety of teaching methods and doing things which students might deem "fun." In fact, many educators state that they rarely get to creatively supplement their classes and are finding it more and more difficult to engage their students.[7] Since student achievement is now measured solely by testing and solely in certain areas of learning such as reading and math, many students are no longer able to express themselves and their passions through means other than book learning and test taking. Essentially, the hands-on approach to learning is all but disappearing.

The problem appears to be that the words "educational reform" have come to mean rigorous testing, standardized curriculum for all students no matter what their desired educational outcomes, more accountability, and other similar "we need more" initiatives. This would be fine if educational reform came about from a consensus among educators about student needs, as well as an understanding about the current economy. Instead, most educational reforms seem to be politically based on the fear that we are no longer up to par when measured against the rest of the world on certain academic measures. And, unfortunately, most reforms are created in summits involving few, if any, actual educators.

One of the newer reforms comes under the heading "College and Career Readiness." Popular thinking is that these two terms are one and the same thing; so many high schools are increasing the high school graduation requirements to align with college entrance requirements in an attempt to help their students be both college and career ready. But sage educators know that college-readiness and career-readiness are not the same.

According to the American Diploma Project, 28% of all college freshman require remediation. In other words, just over a quarter of students have to take high school math and English again in college before they can get on with their college-level classes. In California, 46% of first-year students in the California State University System require remediation.[8] And at one University of California campus, 67% of incoming freshmen have to take remedial math or English courses – and that is at the flagship University of California system! So clearly getting into a university does not mean one is "college ready." As a college Dean of Instruction, I see countless students unprepared for college courses coupled with unrealistic expectations about financial literacy and career awareness. Clearly, recent reforms haven't worked very well.

Standardized testing is not evil, nor are educational reforms. In fact, educators understand the need for assessment and are likely eager to use different methods that help them know what students understand. Teachers are also willingly to try new methods to move students to the next level. But when standardized testing is used to produce a number that in no way recognizes the individual behind the number, we end up with issues. For instance, entire school districts are compared to each other without the individual doing the analysis to ever step foot inside the school or meet an actual student.

Looking at numbers rather than people causes those in charge to create reforms that create competition between districts and among states. In addition to standardized test numbers, high school graduation rates and college attendance rates are also used to compare schools and school districts. With these three numbers ever present, most of the educational reforms that happen push the idea of a 4-year university education as the obvious next step, totally disregarding the needs of the labor market and the skills of the students. Parents are on board with this idea because they still see the university as the main pathway to a better life. But many universities simultaneously espouse that their goal is *not* to prepare students for the workforce, but rather to create critical thinkers.

Instead of considering curriculum as something that stands alone, our educational reforms need to take into account the motivation of students, the skills they will need to be productive in society, the jobs available to those seeking employment, and the diversity and individual needs of each student. If this were to happen, those seeking a 4-year education would find that their courses align better with career opportunities, and those seeking a myriad of additional career paths would also find their needs being met.

AP Classes: The Focus on College Prep

The Orlando Sentinel recently reported an educational issue plaguing Florida's school system: the push from educators for students to take AP classes.[9] As part of the desire to make their schools better, Florida schools are pushing Advanced Placement (AP) and other accelerated courses for a majority of their students. Incentive measures, such as removing class-size requirements and grading high schools higher if they enroll a high number of students in advanced classes, help pave the way for a greater number of students to take the classes.

Although AP classes are not required to graduate, many students take them because their parents and guidance counselors tell them that they should. Some students even find themselves in an AP class despite not signing up for one. This can occur when a counselor finds a student with a high PSAT or SAT score and determines that they would be a good fit for an AP class. In such cases, they sign up the student assuming, based on test scores, that this will be the best fit.

One student personally complained to me, however, that the AP class was simply not worth it. Even though she did well in the class, she did not earn a score on the AP exam that would get her college credit. The College Board considers 3 a passing grade, though nearly 40% of colleges that allow AP credits require a score of 4 or 5. Some colleges, such as Dartmouth College, are planning to stop accepting AP scores entirely.[10] In the student's own words, "the sole purpose of taking the AP class was completely lost."

This is not just a Florida issue. Schools are pushing AP courses across the nation. According to an article in Politico, "Taxpayers have spent hundreds of millions of dollars in recent years to nudge more students into Advanced Placement classes - but a close look at test scores suggests much of the investment has been wasted."[11]

Between 2008 and 2013, the United States government spent $275 million to promote AP classes and help students pay for the exam fees. States have spent millions more.[12] AP enrollment has indeed soared due to these efforts. But enrollment in the course isn't the sole desired outcome. The desired outcome is getting college credit for courses taken in high school. In this measure, even though many community/technical college give credit for AP classes completed, the program overall has failed. In fact, 1.3 million students in the class of 2012 across the nation failed an AP exam with the overall pass rate falling from 61% to 57%.[13]

Eleven other states also incentivize schools to sign up students with things such as extra funds for textbooks, more teacher training, and "best high school" rankings. Low-income students and minority students are given subsidies to take the exams as a way to increase their participation in the AP classes. In August of 2014 alone, over \$29 million was given to states to help subsidize the cost of AP tests.[14]

Proponents of the AP class suggest that simply taking the class is worth it since doing so exposes students to higher expectations and advanced academic coursework. While that may certainly be true, taking an AP class has not been shown to lead to better grades in college level classes, a higher chance of graduating college, or any other tangible benefit besides occasionally, perhaps, maybe, getting college credit.[15] For many, if a student doesn't pass the exam, then taking the AP course was wasted extra effort that could have been directed elsewhere. Locally, AP course completions should be compared to articulated credit, dual credit, and concurrent enrollment, where 100% of students received college credit...but more on that in chapter eight.

Pell Grants: Another Focus on College Prep

Many programs provided by the federal government also encourage traditional college enrollment. One such program is the Pell Grant, which was created to help low-income students to go to college. This grant is not a loan and does not have to be repaid. To apply, a student needs to fill out an application form and grants are awarded based on need. For the 2015-2016 year, the maximum award for a Pell Grant was \$5,775.[16] Though this will not pay for the entire tuition even at most state universities, it certainly does help defray most of the costs.

This is a great program for students who desire to go on to college or the university, and for whom additional formal learning in the classroom is the right answer, especially if the student is unlikely to have the funds for tuition without incurring debt. But, like most educational reform programs, this one steers students towards the university, ignoring the odds that only 7 out of 100 students graduate with a 4-year degree suitable for securing a career that provides for themselves and their family.

Pell Grants also do not begin to address the 73% of students that never make it to a traditional college or university at all. This is because Pell Grants can only be used for education that happens at an accredited college or university, and there are only a few exceptions to this rule. For example, West Virginia and California (along with many other states) allows the Pell Grant for 2-year degree adult technical programs, but not for short-term community college certificate programs. Many one semester, or one year, technical training programs are not eligible. If a student is offered job-based training or an apprenticeship or any other non-accredited educational opportunity, they will most often not qualify for the grant. If a student wants to get a short-term certificate in welding, real estate, or bookkeeping, most financial aid offices tell the student they are not eligible to receive financial assistance through the Pell Grant program. In the eyes of the government, these "alternative" paths are not grant-worthy paths towards employability or self-sufficiency.

I want to be clear in that I believe the Pell Grant program does a lot of good for thousands of students annually...and I am generally not an advocate of non-accredited colleges/universities, especially in light of the many illegal and misleading recruitment tactics of late. But, there are many training solutions that are highly beneficial (such as coding camps, registered apprenticeship programs, as well as very short-term accredited certificate programs), for which I think the utilization of a Pell Grant would be highly beneficial and student-centered.

California A-G: Yet Another Focus on College Prep

Many years ago, The University of California system created what has become known as the A-G subject requirements to help students know what classes to take to be ready to attend a California public university. To be considered for admission to one of the public universities, a student must complete 15 yearlong high school courses with a C or better, with at least 11 of them happening before the senior year in high school.

Here is a list of the requirements:[17]

A) History/social science – 2 years of history/social science including 1 year of world history and one year of US history or US history and Civics.

B) English – 4 years of college-prep English that includes paper writing, as well as the reading of classic and modern literature. Only one English-as-a-Second-Language class can count towards this requirement.

C) Mathematics – 3 years (4 are recommended) of college-prep math including algebra 1 and 2 as well as geometry.

D) Laboratory science – 2 years (3 are recommended) of laboratory science in biology, chemistry, and/or physics.

E) Language other than English – 2 years of the same language other than English.

F) Visual and performing arts – 1 year of visual and performing arts

G) College-preparatory elective – 1 year of additional courses in the areas outlined in A-F

As you can see, this is a stringent list. As an educator, I see no problem with this list for those wishing to attend a 4-year university. I am, however, concerned when the A-G list is no longer used for those wanting to go on to the university but is used instead to be the standard for every student graduating from some high schools (which does occasionally occur).

Looking at the list, you will see that many of these classes would be occupationally useless for someone with a goal to get a 2-year degree in welding, a skilled trade, or landscape architecture. Most of these classes are also not very relevant for certifications such as Process Automation or Hemodialysis Technicians. Yet, students who know they are not going to go the 4-year university path find that they are required to take courses that will not help them prepare for the career of their choice.

The Los Angeles School District has even begun allowing students to get D's in the A to G classes and still graduate from high school. If students were required to get a C or better, the graduation rate would be around 50%.[18] Forcing a college-ready curriculum on all students simply means that most students are neither college nor career ready at graduation.

I'm not picking on California. Most states have rigorous standards for entering college. Many of these states also find that these standards become the "norm" when presenting a high school education plan to students.

While writing this book, I became aware of the UC Curriculum Integration (UCCI) Institute that seeks to integrate general education classes with relevant career and technical education content. With 68 courses on the UCCI course list at the time of this book's publishing, I am optimistic that such work can continue to infuse CTE and general education together. Having CTE courses meeting the A-G requirements may certainly be a step in the right direction. But let us not conflate the issue and falsely assume that classifying all CTE courses into a university-bound A-G structure is in the best interest of all our students.

North Carolina's Future Ready Occupational Track: An Equal Alternative

One state that seems to be appropriately trying to undo the "college for all" educational planning for high school students is North Carolina. Students entering the 9th grade can determine to take one of two tracks: Future-Ready Core for those wanting to attend a 4-year university and Future-Ready Occupational for those going directly to a career or gaining further education leading to a career through the community college system or other educational opportunity. Here are the requirements for either pathway:

North Carolina

Content	Future-Ready Core	Future-Ready Occupational
English	4	4
Mathematics	4	3
Science	3	2
Social Studies	4	2
*World Language	0	0
Health and PE	1	1
Electives	6	6**
CTE	0	4
Fine Arts	0	0
Total	22	22

*2 credits are required of admission into the UNC system
**Includes Occupation Prep I, II, III, IV which includes 300 hours of school-based training, 240 hours of community-based training, and 360 hours of paid employment

You'll note that one significant difference is that Future-Ready Occupational students can gain four CTE courses to expand their employability skills as opposed to university-bound students who receive none. The NC Board of Education website states:

> "Over the past few years, the State Board of Education has changed graduation requirements to better reflect the skills and knowledge students need for success in the workplace, and in community colleges, colleges, and universities. Our goal is for students to be prepared for whatever they want to do after high school graduation."[19]

This demonstrates a viable alternatives can co-exist. California should consider doing something similar to allow students a choice instead of the default A-G prescription. North Carolina is off a great start and the first graduating class with these new standards was just in 2015. At the time of publication the numbers are not out yet determining how many students used which pathway. Conversations with educators in North Carolina, however, leads one to believe that having two equal and viable alternatives for students to choose will open up academic options and expand student success statewide.

Government Refocus to CTE

At the federal level, the academic pendulum is starting to swing back towards the middle. In June of 2015, the US Presidential Scholars program expanded to include scholars in CTE rather than just college-bound honors students. Established in 1964, the program was expanded to include art students in 1979 and now will honor the full gambit of high school students. However, all is not equal. For college-bound students, the program recognizes two high school seniors from each state plus 15 scholars at large. For the arts, only 20 students are recognized and the same will hold true for CTE students. Nonetheless, it is a start.

Yet, at the same time, the Carl D. Perkins Career and Technical Education Act (Perkins) has not been renewed by Congress. This act provides over $1 billion each year to state education programs that support CTE. Without reauthorization, these funds will stop. And then there are the state government cuts. Despite the growing evidence that four-year university programs serve fewer and fewer of our students; states continue to cut vocational programs.

In 2013, for example, the Los Angeles Unified School District, with more than 600,000 students, made plans to cut almost all of its CTE programs by the end of the year. The justification, of course, is budgetary. Programs such as auto body technology, aviation maintenance, audio production, healthcare and photography are expensive to operate.

Similarly, a budget cut in Arizona is leaving CTE classes bruised and battered. The legislature passed a budget that cut funding to these programs by $29 million, assuring that about 30% of the CTE instructors will be cut.[20]

Kansas school districts are also seeing a cut in their 2012 initiative to enhance career and technical education. Senate Bill 155 had the state helping to pay tuition for high school students enrolled in CTE. The school districts also got a $1,000 incentive for each high school student who graduated with an industry-recognized credential in a high-need occupation. The program is working, increasing the number of students taking CTE courses by around 7,000 students and increasing certificates by almost 1,000. Nonetheless, with budget shortfalls, CTE programs get the ax first. This year, Kansas school districts will get less than half the incentive they received last year.[21]

But in a situation where 70% of high school students do not go to college, nearly half of those who do go fail to graduate, and over half of the graduates are unemployed or underemployed, is vocational education really expendable? Or is it the smartest investment we could make in our children, our businesses, and our country's economic future?

As is the case with CTE programs, steps both forward and backward continually take place. Helping our elected officials understand the need for CTE continues to be vital.

An International Comparison

For every young person in America, whatever their background, one of the essential purposes of schooling should be to help them develop the knowledge and skills needed to search for and obtain work that they find satisfying.[22] But instead, when students finally make it into a college classroom, most arrive without any career direction or idea of what they want to get out of their collegiate education. They amass an insane amount of student debt taking classes that have little application to their future goals, and far too often with no credential to show for their efforts.

By comparison, the Swiss education model uses a nationwide system that matches high school students with training, jobs, and education which keeps their older teenagers engaged. The Swiss have made learning to work and learning about work central to their education system. Many 16-year-olds in Switzerland already have secured apprenticeships embedded within their schooling. This has resulted in a youth unemployment rate below four percent.[23]

One school in Indiana has begun using the German model for some of its industry certifications.[24] After speaking with companies in the area, Ivy Tech Community College realized that companies needed to train 4-year graduates at a high cost with no guarantee that these employees would stay with the firm. Even then, they were having trouble finding enough people to apply.

So, Ivy Tech Community College began using the German model of career and technical education to keep up with the demand for skilled workers. It is a dual system of education and training that combines classroom instruction with on-the-job apprenticeships designed to lead to full-time positions. The employers pay 75% of the annual cost of trainee and the government covers the rest.[25] Upon completion, the German students receive a credential called a certification qualification.

In Germany, this particular setup has kept youth unemployment down to 7.7 percent in 2014[26], which is less than the 12.2 percent unemployment in the United States.[27] To catch up with Germany, the US would have to add 2.5 million apprenticeships to the 358,000 that currently exist.

Similarly, the UK government has pledged to create 3 million apprenticeships by 2020, including 2,000 degree apprenticeships to start within a year. Degree apprenticeships allow students to complete paid work at an accredited company while studying for a degree in a management-related subject at the same time. Several prestigious companies have signed up for degree apprenticeship programs which give students three years in the workplace, a degree from a university business school, and a professional qualification as a chartered manager. Using this model, students earn a salary while completing school and they do not pay tuition fees!

Then there is Singapore. It has one of the most competitive economies in the world because of its close linkage between education and economic development. All of the government, including the finance ministry, economic development board, manpower ministry, education ministry, urban and environmental planning bodies, and housing and immigration authorities study where they want their economy to grow, and then they educate a workforce around that vision.

Currently, Singapore is looking to be a scientific hub. They identify critical needs and project demands, and then they channel that information into training and continuing education. They believe it helps them move faster into growing sectors, reduces the oversupply of jobs no longer needing workers, and helps students and the government spend money more effectively on education. The end result is that Singapore is ready to meet the demands to be the scientific hub they planned to become.

Enrollment in CTE classes in Singapore has doubled since 1995, with CTE students making up about 25% of the secondary education population. Additionally, 82% of the students were placed into jobs with strong pay levels upon graduation. In Singapore, however, these students remain in school getting a CTE education and decent paying jobs. They only have a 2.5% dropout rate.[28] Comparatively, in the U.S., over one-fourth of students drop out of high school as quantified in chapter two.

What does all of this tell us? The United States desperately needs to find a way to close the skills gap, and part of the answer may already be working elsewhere. Refining our approach will help both employers and students who aren't winning on the one-way-to-win pathway.

The Reinvention of Schools

Not all schools are stuck in the one-size-fits-all paradigm and are offering different ways to win. Let's look a few to get a feel for what is possible and what is working.

Brooklyn, New York has created a high school called Pathways in Technology Early College. Instead of a 4-year high school, P-Tech is a 6 year school offering both a high school diploma and an associate's degree. The focus of the degree is either computer science or engineering. Students don't just take classes to get a diploma, however. Instead, the school has partnered with IBM, City University, NYC College of Technology, and the NYC Department of Education to offer paid internships with tech companies. This work experience is proving invaluable as the first class readies itself for graduation in 2017. Six students have already graduated early and half of them are working for IBM. The focus at P-Tech is job-ready skills, with students having a goal and a plan to reach that goal.

Then there is e3 Civic Charter High School. Conveniently located inside the San Diego Public Library, students have access to over one million books, as well as the auditorium, art gallery, and learning space. Classrooms constantly take on a new look with furniture on wheels, allowing students to create groupings that fit each learning situation. These high school students are able to take a wide variety of classes that expose them to career fields currently looking for employees. These classes include those in medical biology, biotech, and bio-engineering. Once again, the focus is not on graduation rates or test scores, but on real life experiences and job-ready skills.

Toledo Technology Academy (TTA) comprises grades 7-12 and students graduating from TTA acquire specific industry certifications while in school and can enter into jobs in engineering and manufacturing when they graduate. TTA does not have a separate vocational/technical track. All students are expected to complete both academic and technical classes, including honors or articulation classes. TTA has strong partnerships with local businesses, allowing their technical training to be relevant to local jobs.

Finally, let's look at an entire school district near Denver, Colorado. Mapleton School District[29] was not known for its graduation rate. In fact, 50% of its students never received a diploma. So, when Charlotte Ciancio became the new superintendent, she shook things up a bit.

After touring the country looking for appropriate educational models, she came home and created 17 distinct programs, including seven high schools instead of just one. Each program was created to help a different type of student. For instance, those that like to learn on their own can go to Welby New Tech. At Welby, teachers never lecture for more than 15 minutes and students are busy on computers and doing their own projects. For students wanting even more flexibility, they might want to consider Connections Academy. This is an online K-12 public school that allows students to attend from home or another location outside a traditional classroom.

If these aren't for you, you might consider Mapleton Expeditionary School for the Arts (MESA). MESA is a college prep school that allows students to investigate real-world issues and use what they learn to make positive change in their community. For those students who want a more traditional approach, they can attend York International, which is a K-12 school. This is the perfect school for families that want to be involved in their children's education and would like a private school atmosphere.

To date, it is impossible to know whether these ideas will lead kids to employment in a way that best suits their needs. But what is interesting is that school systems are starting to listen to the cries of foul from those that have followed the traditional path and found it wanting.

---

1 https://www.law.cornell.edu/supremecourt/text/268/510

2 *Public Education in the United States.* Microsoft Encarta Online Encyclopedia 2001.

3 A Nation at Risk: The Imperative for Educational Reform, A Report to the Nation and the Secretary of Education United States Department of Education by The National Commission on Excellence in Education. April 1983. http://datacenter.spps.org/uploads/sotw_a_nation_at_risk_1983.pdf

4 A Nation at Risk: The Imperative for Educational Reform, A Report to the Nation and the Secretary of Education United States Department of Education by The National Commission on Excellence in Education. April 1983. http://datacenter.spps.org/uploads/sotw_a_nation_at_risk_1983.pdf

5 Morton, B. Q., & Dalton, B. (2007). Changes in instructional hours in four subjects by public school teachers of grades 1 through 4. Washington, DC: U.S. Department of Education, National Center for Education Statistics. Retrieved from http://nces.ed.gov/pubs2007/2007305.pdf Perie, M., Baker, D. P., & Bobbitt, S. A. (1997). Time spent teaching core academic subjects in elementary schools: Comparisons across community, school, teacher, and student characteristics (NCES 97-293). Washington, DC: U.S. Department of Education, National Center for Education Statistics. Retrieved from http://nces.ed.gov/pubs/97293.pdf

6 McMurrer, J. (2007). Choices, changes, and challenges: Curriculum and instruction in the NCLB era. Washington, DC: Center on Education Policy.

7 Valli, L., & Buese, D. (2007). The changing roles of teachers in an era of high-stakes accountability. American Educational Research Journal, 44(3), 519–558.

8 Source: Pamela Clute, a UCR math professor and assistant vice provost for academic partnerships. (As quoted in The Riverside Press-Enterprise. *Education: Battle on to increase graduation, college-going rates.* Sunday, October 30, 2011).

9 Orlando Sentinel. Martin, Annie. Students taking too many tough courses, some say. September 29, 2015. http://www.orlandosentinel.com/features/education/os-more-students-advanced-courses-20150929-story.html#

10 http://www.npr.org/sections/thetwo-way/2013/01/17/169637369/ap-credit-will-no-longer-be-accepted-at-dartmouth

11 Politico. Simon, Stephanie. AP classes failing students. August 21, 2013. http://www.politico.com/story/2013/08/education-advanced-placement-classes-tests-095723#

12 Politico. Simon, Stephanie. AP classes failing students. August 21, 2013. http://www.politico.com/story/2013/08/education-advanced-placement-classes-tests-095723#

13 College Board 10th Annual Report to the Nation. February, 2014. http://apreport.collegeboard.org/

14 http://www.marketplace.org/2015/05/04/education/learning-curve/changing-role-advanced-placement-classes

15 Trevor Packer, Senior Vice President of College Board. http://www.politico.com/story/2013/08/education-advanced-placement-classes-tests-095723#

16 US Department of Education. Office of Federal Student Aid. https://studentaid.ed.gov/sa/types/grants-scholarships/pell

17 University of California A-G Subject Requirements. http://www.ucop.edu/agguide/a-g-requirements/

18 http://www.latimes.com/local/education/la-me-lausd-20150610-story.html

19 NC State Board of Education, Department of Public Instruction. High School Graduation Requirements. http://www.dpi.state.nc.us/docs/curriculum/home/graduationrequirements.pdf

20 http://www.trivalleycentral.com/coolidge_examiner/education/state-budget-cuts-threaten-cavit-s-future/article_3ba5d85c-92e8-11e5-a3e5-6f36b3437549.html

21 http://www.kansas.com/news/local/education/article25701169.html#storylink=cpy

22 Hoffman, Nancy. (Nov 2015). High school in Switzerland blends work with learning. The Phi Delta Kappan, vol. 97 *no. 3 29-33.* Phi Delta Kappa International. http://pdk.sagepub.com/content/97/3/29.full?ijkey=mbwHvmbtrQ7sg&keytype=ref&siteid=sppdk.

23 Hoffman, Nancy. (Nov 2015). High school in Switzerland blends work with learning. The Phi Delta Kappan, vol. 97 *no. 3 29-33.* Phi Delta Kappa International. http://pdk.sagepub.com/content/97/3/29.full?ijkey=mbwHvmbtrQ7sg&keytype=ref&siteid=sppdk.

24 http://www.pbs.org/newshour/updates/educate-americans-jobs-ask-germans-employers-urge/

25 http://www.publications.parliament.uk/pa/ld200607/ldselect/ldeconaf/138/13807.htm

26 http://dw.com/p/1GD9B

27 http://www.bls.gov/news.release/youth.nr0.htm

28 Case Study on Institute of Technical Education (ITE), APEC, 2010. Accessed on January 26, 2012: http://www.apecknowledgebank.org/file.aspx?id=2403).

29 http://www.mapleton.us/

CHAPTER 4

WHAT COLOR IS YOUR COLLAR?

The Alternative to What?

For years, schools have pushed the idea of a 4-year university education in order to get a high-paying white collar job. Any other pathway was coined an alternative and usually said with a sigh. Those on the "alternative" path were not candidates for the university, but still, we had to do something with them, right?

But let's review the numbers one more time. Only 7 out of 100 students make it on the path we are pushing. A mere 7% find the one way to be the right way. That leaves 93% of our students floundering for a wide variety of reasons. So, shouldn't we ask ourselves why vocational education or career and technical education (CTE) or any other form of secondary education other than a bachelor's degree is the "alternative"? (Note: in some states the term *alternative* indicates the students attending a school are there due to behavioral challenges or their discipline history, but I am using the term in this chapter to indicate something that is not preferred, less than, or the second choice).

What exactly is alternative about what a majority of students need, what a majority of high-paying occupations require, and what is in high-demand in most industries? When did being a skilled craftsman or technician become the alternative? More importantly, why did being a skilled craftsman or technician become the alternative?

While we are asking, let's look at what it is an alternative to: which is frequently unemployment, underemployment, and excessive student debt. It would seem that we need to come up with another label. Rather than seeing the one-way-to-win and the alternative, we should be offering our students several, equally viable ways to be successful after high school – with each pathway dependent on their individual skills, abilities, and goals with the outcome of being employed in a field that brings all students a measure of happiness.

Plumbers vs Philosophers

If you were to take a poll of 100 random strangers in your community asking them which was a better college major, plumbing or philosophy, you would probably find that most people would pick philosophy. If you asked them why, you are likely to hear messages that resonate with the idea of white collar workers vs. blue collar workers.

White collar workers typically perform professional, managerial, or administrative work in an office environment. In general, these jobs are less physically laborious and are historically seen to have higher pay than those in blue collar positions. This belief has been further fueled by the notion that America is a "knowledge-based economy." Additionally, those with white collar jobs typically have university degrees.

On the other hand, a blue collar worker is thought to be a member of the working class. They perform some type of manual labor that can either be skilled or unskilled. These jobs are frequently in manufacturing, mining, construction, mechanical, maintenance, and technical, as well as a myriad of other areas. Blue collar workers typically work outside of an office environment and have a wide pay-scale for their work. Though some blue collar workers are paid more than those in white collar jobs, people feel blue collar workers are often paid less for doing harder work.

So, what would the people taking your survey say about philosophy vs plumbing? They might let you know that a philosopher gets to sit in an academic office and contemplate life while bringing in the big bucks, while the plumber would be underneath sinks and houses, dealing with clogged toilets while bringing in an hourly pittance.

Do you think they would be right? Is it better to be one over the other? Is there more intrinsic value to being a philosopher? To help us answer this question, I will refer to John Gardner, an educator and politician. In his book *Excellence* he says:

"The society which scorns excellence in plumbing because plumbing is a humble activity and tolerates shoddiness in philosophy because it is an exalted activity will have neither good plumbing nor philosophy. Neither its pipes nor its theories will hold water."[1]

Isn't this the truth? Society has somehow degraded the skilled technician or craftsman as being something less – something not to be desired. Imagine being around the Thanksgiving table and someone says, "Oh, Jonny, I hear you are going to college. What do you plan to be?" Jonny says, "Oh, I'm at the university studying botany." Everyone is typically impressed and says how great that is! Now, they move on to Susie. "And Susie, how about you? What are you going to do after high school?" Susie says that she is going to learn precision tool making and go into manufacturing. Inevitably, faces visibly fall and people stammer. Eventually, someone says, "Oh, well, that sounds interesting…hopefully someday you'll figure it all out."

Our society has stopped embracing those people that keep our society going. In the past two generations, we have villainized the skilled trades and began calling them "alternatives." The philosophy majors that are $150,000 in debt but working at a dead-end cubical job for $32,000 a year are deemed the successful ones. The plumber, with no school debt, and a starting of $36,000 with the potential to make over $80,000 a year will hopefully "figure it out someday."[2] Honestly, this just doesn't make any sense to me.

Imagine Life With Only White Collar Workers

I read a great book recently by Mike Rowe called *Profoundly Disconnected*. If you are this far into my book you definitely should buy his also. In it, he makes a confession that I believe most of us should make. He admits that he is addicted to civilized society.[3] Aren't we all? Do any of us want to go back to outhouses, no running water, cooking on a wood stove, or riding through town on a mule? Probably not.

Using numerous stories, Mike Rowe colorfully paints a picture explaining that white collar, blue collar, and middle-skilled workers are all necessary to living in a civilized society. To prove this point, let's imagine life with no skilled tradesmen and only white collar workers.

Imagine that Mr. White Collar gets up in the morning and heads to the shower. For reasons completely unknown to him, there is no hot water this particular morning. He'd call the plumber, but this is White Collar World and there are no plumbers. After a brisk shower, he heads into the kitchen to make himself a cup of coffee. He flips the switch and nothing happens. After repeating this several times, he realizes that something must be wrong with the outlet. He'd call the electrician, but this is White Collar World and there are no electricians.

Skipping his cup of coffee, he heads to the garage and jumps into his sporty car. About 5 miles from home, his car stops running. He opens the hood but sees nothing obviously wrong. He'd call a mechanic, but this is White Collar World and there are no mechanics. He now finds himself several miles from both work and home. Should he take the bus or a taxi? Oh, wait, he can't take either because there are no bus or taxi drivers. He does what he must and walks to work.

Arriving over an hour late, Mr. White Collar fires up his computer and sets to work. He's written a great business proposal and is all ready to print it out for his boss when it disappears. He looks in his files and in the trash bin of his computer. It is nowhere. It is time to call for some computer help. But wait. There are no computer technicians...

Are you starting to get the picture?

However, even this fable isn't entirely accurate. There are no garbage collectors in White Collar World so the communities are filled with stinky trash. There are no sewer maintenance technicians either, so the sewer systems are no longer working and sewage is backing up onto the roadways. Speaking of roads, there are no road construction workers, so potholes the size of Rhode Island are forming, which really isn't a problem because, without mechanics, the cars won't go for long anyway.

But let's take it a step further. Remember the coffee maker that wouldn't work for Mr. White Collar? Without factory workers, there is no coffee maker to break down. Nor is there a car or a computer which both rely on skilled technicians to manufacture. Even the clothes Mr. White Collar is wearing would cease to exist.

Listening only to the one-way-to-win philosophy would leave us with millions of university graduates...but no roads, no utilities, no clean water, and no food. We'd have no one to build a new home for us. There would be no one working in manufacturing facilities or distribution centers. Even our hospitals would be devoid of those that do a majority of the work.

In his preface, Mike Rowe says, "I had lost my connection to honest work. I was no longer mindful of the miracle of modern plumbing, or food production, or domestic manufacturing, or cheap electricity."[4]

It appears that those running our education system have the same problem. But, keep reading. I believe there is hope. The next few chapters will begin to highlight some proposed solutions and share ways to think about our educational system more holistically.

---

1 Excellence. John w. Gardner. 1995
2 http://www.payscale.com/research/US/Job=Plumber/Hourly_Rate#
3 Profoundly Disconnected: A True Confession. Mike Rowe. 2014. p 3
4 Profoundly Disconnected: A True Confession. Mike Rowe. 2014. p xxvi

CHAPTER 5

LABOR MARKET REALITIES

Then and Now

I n 1960, when taking into account all jobs in the American economy, 20% required a 4-year degree or higher, 20% were technical jobs requiring skilled training, and 60% were classified as unskilled.[1] But what's the right percentage to meet the labor market demand for tomorrow? In 2018, Harvard University predicts only 33% of all jobs will require a 4-year degree or more while the overwhelming majority will be middle-skilled jobs requiring technical skills and training at the credential or Associates Degree level.[2]

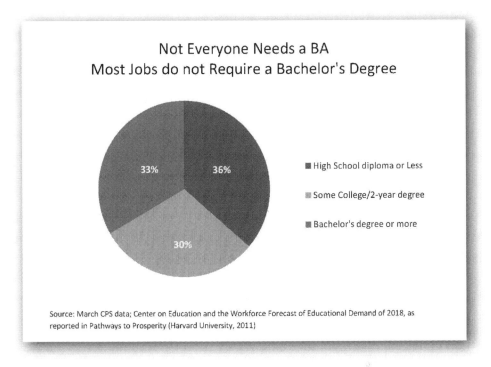

Not Everyone Needs a BA
Most Jobs do not Require a Bachelor's Degree

- 33%
- 36%
- 30%

- High School diploma or Less
- Some College/2-year degree
- Bachelor's degree or more

Source: March CPS data; Center on Education and the Workforce Forecast of Educational Demand of 2018, as reported in Pathways to Prosperity (Harvard University, 2011)

Well-intentioned attempts to send more and more students straight to the university will not change the types of jobs that dominate our economy, nor will a "college-for-all" mentality mask these labor market realities.[3] As mentioned, the "college for all" rhetoric that has been so much a part of the current education reform movement is often interpreted as "university for all." This message needs to be significantly broadened to, "a post-high school credential for all."[4]

Students at various educational levels have left school without employable skills, setting them up for failure, and costing them and taxpayers millions.[5] At the same time, the labor market is desperate for highly-trained, skilled technicians.[6]

The Car Accident

With a primary focus on 4-year university degrees and the jobs that require them, I think we forget how many people work in jobs that are highly-skilled but require less than a bachelor's degree. While the fictitious story of White Collar World in the previous chapter pokes fun at the extreme of a world with only white collar workers, this concept really came into clear focus for me when my wife was in a car accident.

The first person involved in her care was the 911 dispatcher. Dispatchers need to graduate from high school but often find it helpful to have higher level classes in criminal justice, communications, emergency management, or public safety protocols. According to the Bureau of Labor and Statistics, 911 operators earn an average salary nationally of $37,460 a year.[7]

Next, on the scene came the police officer. Depending upon the department/county, officers need to graduate from high school and then go on to a police academy where they are trained. Some also require college courses in subjects such as criminal justice, criminology, evidence gathering, law enforcement strategies, and constitutional rights. The average wage for a police officer is $48,366.[8]

Shortly after the officer came onto the scene, the Emergency Medical Technician (EMT) and paramedics arrived. To be a paramedic, one must first get an EMT-B certificate, often from a community/technical college. EMTs start with an EMT-B and then go on to get a 2-year degree in paramedic training. EMTs make $29,987[9] and paramedics make $43,283[10] a year.

Once we arrived at the hospital, my wife had her vital signs taken by a nurse. The nurse had a 4-year degree in nursing and makes $57,619 a year. [11] Then she was whisked off to have a series of x-rays. The x-ray technician had a 2-year degree in x-ray technology and makes on average $41,906[12] a year. In the meantime, a phlebotomist came by to draw blood. She needed a professional certificate (I asked) and makes an average of $30,303[13] a year.

While all this was happening, I was working with hospital billing about our insurance coverage and ability to pay. To work in hospital billing, one must have a certification in medical billing and coding. The average pay for a medical biller in a hospital is $34,932[14] a year.

Eventually, the radiologist read her reports. To be a radiologist, you would need to complete 4 years of college, 4 years of medical school, a one-year internship, four years of residency, and then an exam. Radiologists make $249,055 a year. [15] Several hours later, we saw her doctor, who also had 4 years of college, 4 years of medical school, internships, and residency training. Her annual salary was $206,037.[16]

My point is this: Of the ten people involved with in her trip to the emergency room, only three of them required a 4-year college degree. And, in fact, two of these required far more than that. Every other occupation that helped my wife after her accident were those that got industry certifications or 2-year degrees.

My wife is fine, thankfully, after this event. But the experience taught me something significant about the nature of work in the United States. This is called the 1:2:7 ratio.

The 1:2:7 Ratio

Based on my experience, far more jobs in the healthcare field require certificates and 2-year degrees than those that require 4-year degrees or more. Upon further research, statistics bear this out. For every one doctor employed in the healthcare industry, there are two nurses, and seven other health professionals.

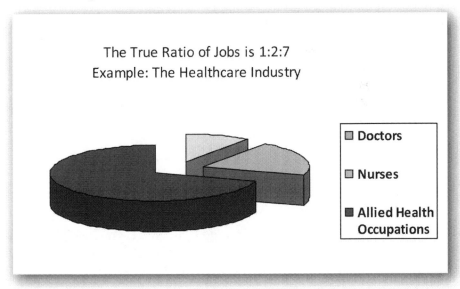

The true ratio of jobs in our economy is 1:2:7.[17] For every occupation that requires a master's degree or more, two professional jobs require a university degree, and there are over half a dozen jobs requiring a 1-year certificate or 2-year degree, and each of these technicians is in very high-skilled areas that are in great demand.[18] In fact, this holds true across all industries (except for government and public education where the 4-year degree is an unreliable proxy for competence). This 1:2:7 ratio was the same in 1950, the same in 1990, and will be the same in 2030.[19]

The US Bureau of Labor and Statistics says the jobs on the following chart will be the fastest growing jobs from 2014 to 2014. Of these jobs, only three require more than a 2-year degree.

America's Fastest Growing Occupations
Forecasted growth in U.S. occupations from 2014 to 2024

	2014		2024	% Growth
Wind turbine service technicians	4,400	▶	9,200	108.0
Occupational therapy assistants	33,000	▶	47,100	42.7
Physical therapist assistants	78,700	▶	110,700	40.6
Physical therapist aides	50,000	▶	69,500	39.0
Home health aides	913,500	▶	1,261,900	38.1
Commercial divers	4,400	▶	6,000	36.9
Nurse practitioners	126,900	▶	171,700	35.2
Physical therapists	210,000	▶	282,700	34.0
Statisticians	30,000	▶	40,100	33.8
Ambulance drivers and attendants	19,600	▶	26,100	33.0

Additionally, baby-boom workers are retiring and leaving lots of openings for millennials. For instance, there are 600,000 jobs for electricians in the country today and about half of these are occupied by soon-to-retire boomers.[20] This could be a big opportunity for the millennial generation. In general, the U.S. is going to need a lot more pipe-fitters, nuclear power plant operators, carpenters, welders, utility workers and more. The problem is that today's students aren't getting the type of training needed to fill these positions.

The hope of many educators is that by encouraging university education, the number of university-trained workers will increase, and thus it is assumed that the demand for their services in the workplace will increase as well. Unfortunately, this is not so. The whole pie may get bigger as the labor force and the economy grow, but the ratio will not change.[21] The reality is there will not be more professional jobs available within the labor market as some professional jobs are replaced by technology and others are being outsourced.[22]

The Highest Paid Game

Looking at the 1:2:7 ratio, many people agree but still believe that they should be one of those getting the high degree while leaving "others" to do the dirty work. Once again, we have brainwashed our students into believing that the careers making the most money are those that require a 4-year university degree or more (such as a Masters degree).

My suspicion is that you may still be relying too heavily on that idea as well. To prove my point, let's play a little game. Following is an income ranking questionnaire. It is based on the State of California's labor market, but is similar across the United States.[24]

Look over the 10 career titles below and rank them in order of their wage/earnings, with number one being the highest income earner, and 10 being the lowest:

Income Ranking (1-10)

_____Air Traffic Controllers

_____Dental Hygienists

_____Electrical Power-Line Installers/Repairers

_____Diagnostic medical sonographers

_____Elevator installers & repairers

_____Geographer

_____Market Research Analysts

_____Writers and Authors

_____Community & Social Service Specialists

_____Mental Health Counselors

No really, go back and do it. Rank them one through ten.

———

How do you feel about your choices? Were you able to easily rank them in order of how much each occupation earns? Try it again with this second listing. Rank these ten jobs in order of their wage/earnings, with number one being the highest income earner, and 10 being the lowest:

_____First-Line Supervisors of Police/Detectives
_____Radiation Therapists
_____Power Distributors & Dispatchers
_____Logistics & Distribution Managers
_____Computer Network Support Specialists
_____Soil and Plant Scientists
_____Anthropologists & Archeologists
_____Athletic Trainers
_____Music Directors & Composers
_____Radio & Television Announcers

How well do you think you did with this second set? Most people actually struggle with this exercise because we never actually spend time learning about the real wages of different occupations in our local region. We may have preconceived notions about what jobs pay better than others, but our beliefs are often shaped by our personal experiences and not necessarily labor market data. I have completed this activity with thousand of educators and parents over the years. When asked to rank them, most intelligent folks can't rank these 10 occupations in the correct order. So, don't feel bad if you don't get them right.

Well, unless you have listed them in the order they appear, one through 10, you are wrong. These occupations are already listed in the correctly ranked order based on their average annual wage in California.[24] And now, let's look at the final piece of the puzzle. Write down to the right of each occupational title what you think is the needed education level for each of these jobs. You may use a clean version of this activity on Appendix C. For those that want a little help, a completed questionnaire wage answers and education required is included for you in Appendix D.

If you look closely at this ranking, you will see that the first five careers in each set require an associate's degree or less yet they pay more than the next five careers which require a bachelor's degree or more. This is why we can no longer show a diagram stating that the more education you get the better off you will be financially. This is simply no longer the truth. At this point, you may be experiencing what researcher call cognitive dissonance. The facts and your perceived reality may be out of alignment. It may be hard to initially accept, but many occupations requiring hands-on skills and industry certifications do in fact command a higher wage than many other jobs which require a 4-year degree. In the 21st century economy, skills and experience often trump degrees.

What Current Data Shows

In 2013, College Measures worked to link student data with wage data in five states in hopes to help people make wise decisions about postsecondary education. Some of the results were surprising to the mainstream public, but are exactly what millennials have been learning by experience, and it's what I've been saying for years.[25]

Comparison of Credentials Awarded in U.S. from 2008 and 2012

	Certificates Less than 1-year	Certificates of 1 but less than 2-years	Associate's Degree	Bachelor's Degree	Master's Degree
2008	265,454	183,483	732,432	1,554,843	625,002
2012	337,870	286,825	1,017,446	1,778,598	754,229
Growth	27.3%	56.3%	38.9%	15.0%	20.7%

One of the results was that short-term higher education credentials are worth as much as long-term degrees. In fact, institutions of higher learning granted almost as many certificates and 2-year degrees compared to universities granting 4-year bachelor's degrees. These sub-baccalaureate credentials are the fastest growing segment in educational awards offered.[26]

What is even more interesting is that the average first-year earnings of associate's degree graduates are higher than the earnings of those with bachelor's degrees. For instance, Texas graduates with a technical-oriented Associate's degree will earn $11,000 more the first year than someone with a bachelor's degree.[27]

This actually reminds me of a joke. A lawyer hires a plumber to come and fix his toilet. The plumber works for two hours, fixes the toilet, and hands the lawyer a bill. The lawyer takes a step back, adjusts his glasses, looks at the bill again, and exclaims, "My gosh, man! You've charged more per hour than me, and I'm a lawyer!" The humble plumber takes a step back, wipes his brow, and says, "I know, sir. That was my problem when I was a lawyer, too." We all need to learn, or be reminded, that earning additional degrees does not always correlate with bringing home a higher salary.

In addition to 2-year degrees, certificates are also being granted in high numbers with 600,000 granted in 2013. The College Measures study shows that the longer certificates, those ranging from 1 to 2 years, offer a viable alternative to an associate's degree and can also offer the holder high first-year earnings.[28] At the present time, the certificates most in demand are those in manufacturing, construction, and health-related fields. Once again, in Texas, students completing certificates in Communication Systems Installation and Repair Technology earn $78,515 a year versus the average $40,000 of someone with a general bachelor's degree.[29]

Another big finding of the College Measures study is that what you study is more important than where you study. Technical and occupational skills are rewarded more than many of the coveted liberal arts degrees in the "-ologies". The idea that one should just get a 4-year degree in anything is no longer valid as the default pathway to success.

Additionally, another finding suggests that the popular acronym STEM (science, technology, engineering, and math) should actually be TEM. Although some people push the science part of STEM, the labor market data does not indicate a premium for science degrees. Instead, the higher wages are going to those with degrees in technology, engineering, and math. Once again, looking at Texas, we see that a 2-year degree in computer and information sciences and in mechanical engineering earns around $30,000 to start. But those with an associate's in biology, chemistry, or math earn less than $20,000. The same holds true for STEM bachelor's degrees, with those in mechanical engineering earning $74,000 while those with a chemistry degree only earns $36,000.[30]

The world does need more scientists, but the truth about occupations in the sciences is that many simply do not need the skills learned in a traditional science classes at the 2-year or 4-year level. For most jobs in the sciences, a Masters program is where the actual employability skills are taught. Moreover, about twice as many jobs require welding as a background skill for employment than jobs which require background skills in chemistry.[31] Nonetheless, nearly every school invests in expensive chemistry labs and requires chemistry courses despite the fact that welding provides a better science class with context for science principles while teaching an occupational skill. (Thankfully in California, many UCCI courses support this idea).

This study really shows the misguided idea that there is only one way to win. Rather than thinking about technical degrees as "alternatives," we need to recognize that technical degrees help students get good-paying jobs that are in demand. If one goal of education is to help a student get a good job, then snubbing "alternative" paths and underfunding technical programs in our schools has got to stop.

The Jobless Millennials

In 2013, only 27% of college grads landed a job in a field related to their major. But around 60% landed a job requiring a degree. In 2014, only 51% of college graduates landed jobs that required degrees, down nearly 10% from the year before.[32]

After spring graduation in 2015, 2.8 million graduates with bachelor's, master's, and doctoral degrees, were ready to begin work.[33] Unemployment was at its lowest rate in seven years, giving the graduates a feeling that all was right with the world. As it turns out, things were just as bad as they have been for years with millennials making up 40% of the unemployed in the United States.[34] In fact, looking at the Bureau of Labor and Statistics, millennials have been in the longest period of unemployment since World War II.

Most of these unemployed millennials have a college education, but have found that the promised rewards of a good paying job are not being fulfilled, and the cost of getting the education is getting higher. One study shows that the volume of student loans increased 77% from 2002 to 2012.[35] Therefore, this means that those entering into the job market come with large student loans but are not finding a job that will pay their bills and pay down their debt.

Are these students getting what they paid for? According to a survey by the Higher Education Research Institute, 88% of freshman entering college say that the most important reason to go to college is to get a good job.[36] Yet, these same students are finding no jobs available when they graduate. The rising cost of college, along with low-wage jobs for graduates, indicates that a college education may not be the investment it used to be.

In addition to those that can't find employment are those that find themselves in gray-collar jobs. The Economic Policy Institute suggests that 14.99% of new graduates are underemployed.[37] However, the measure of underemployment only measures what is known as underutilization, meaning it measures those in part-time work that wish to have full-time work. This number does not reflect education-based underemployment which includes those with college degrees working in jobs that don't require one (e.g. waitress, bartender, Uber driver). In fact, 46% of college graduates were working in a job that did not require their degree in 2014.[38]

Now, academics love to debate the purpose of higher education, and there is an argument to be made that vocational preparation should not be the desired goal upon graduation...but it is. See Chapter six for a more thorough dive into this topic. Regardless of one's ideological leaning, I think everyone can agree that we want students to make informed decisions about their education, and that we all want students to be happy and successful in their multiple future careers.

In the past, when a student graduated and couldn't find work, they often went back to school to further their education. Going back meant getting another bachelor's or moving on to get a master's degree or doctorate. Now, however, a reverse is occurring. Many university graduates are going back to school at a community college in order to get an employable skill set.

According to the American Association of Community Colleges, 1 in 14 people who attend a community college already have a bachelor's degree. Some community colleges have as many as 1 in 5.[39] Most of those that return are looking to upgrade their skills, get specialized skills, or to prepare for a career, which is something their university degree perhaps didn't do. A 2014 study from the Community College Research Center showed that two-year colleges are providing increasingly higher economic returns for graduates over the last three decades.[40] Illustrative of this point, one community college in West Virginia recently reported that the fastest growing segment of their student population were people with Masters degrees coming back to the community college to gain technical skills!

Now try to imagine these unemployed and underemployed millennials with the proper career and education guidance. Is it possible that if they had been guided to careers that matched their skills and desires with occupations that were actually in demand that they would be happily employed at this time? The answer is, yes! A substantial number of these graduates could be happily employed in excellent jobs had they secured appropriate skills during their academic tenure.

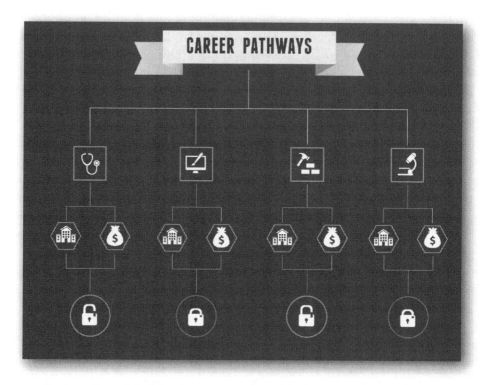

Rather than going back to get an associate's or certificate in a career that is hiring, many students could have started there, been employed, and found themselves without substantial debt. The new labor market reality is this: a degree in just anything is no longer the key to a good job as it once was. Unless a student has a career path that includes a 4-year university education requirement, they might be better served (at least initially) to look at the many other pathways available.

---

1 Project Lead the Way (www.pltw.org). And: GetReal (www.getrealca.com).

2 90% of all jobs in the future will require some education and training beyond high school according to: The National Science Foundation (2012) PI Conference keynote by Jane Oates, Assistant Secretary ETA, Department of Labor. And: Symonds, W., Schwartz, R., & Ferguson, R. (February 2011). *Pathways to Prosperity: Meeting the Challenge of Preparing Young Americans for the 21st Century.* Report issued by the Pathways to Prosperity Project, Harvard Graduate School of Education. And: Deil-Amen & DeLuca. (2010). *The Underserved Third: How our Educational Structures Populate an Educational Underclass.* Routledge. And: The Bureau of Labor Statistics, Occupational Outlook Handbook, 2010-2011 Edition. And: The Workforce Alliance. (2009). *California's Forgotten Middle-Skill Jobs: Meeting the Demands of a 21st Century Economy.* Washington DC.

3 Deil-Amen & DeLuca. (2010). *The Underserved Third: How our Educational Structures Populate an Educational Underclass.* Routledge.

4 Symonds, W., Schwartz, R., & Ferguson, R. (February 2011). *Pathways to Prosperity: Meeting the Challenge of Preparing Young Americans for the 21st Century.* Report issued by the Pathways to Prosperity Project, Harvard Graduate School of Education.

5 Fleming, K. (April 2012), *The Inland Empire's Neglected Majority: By the Numbers.* Paper presented at California Community College Association for Occupational Educational. Costa Mesa, CA. And: Symonds, W., Schwartz, R., & Ferguson, R. (February 2011). *Pathways to Prosperity: Meeting the Challenge of Preparing Young Americans for the 21st Century.* Report issued by the Pathways to Prosperity Project, Harvard Graduate School of Education. And: The Workforce Alliance. (2009). *California's Forgotten Middle-Skill Jobs: Meeting the Demands of a 21st Century Economy.* Washington DC. And: Scott, J., and Sarkees-Wircenski, M. (2004). *Overview of Career and Technical Education: Third Edition.* Homewood, Illinois: American Technical Publishers, Inc.

6 Carnevale, A., Jayasundera, T., & Hanson, A. (2012). *Career & Technical Education: Five Ways that Pay along the Way to the B.A.* Center on Education and the Workforce, Georgetown University. And: The Workforce Alliance. (2009). *California's Forgotten Middle-Skill Jobs: Meeting the Demands of a 21st Century Economy.* Washington DC. And: Gray, K. & Herr, E. (2006). *Other Ways to Win: Creating Alternatives for High School Graduates. Third Edition.* Thousand Oaks: Corwin Press.

7 Bureau of Labor and Statistics. 2013

8 http://www.payscale.com/research/US/Job=Police_Officer/Salary

9 http://www.payscale.com/research/US/Job=Emergency_Medical_Technician_(EMT)_-_Basic/Hourly_Rate

10 http://www.payscale.com/research/US/Job=Paramedic/Hourly_Rate

11 http://www.payscale.com/research/US/Job=Registered_Nurse_(RN)/Hourly_Rate

12 http://www.payscale.com/research/US/Job=X-Ray_Technician/Hourly_Rate

13 http://www.payscale.com/research/US/Job=Phlebotomist/Hourly_Rate

14 http://www.payscale.com/research/US/Job=Medical_Billing%2fCoding_Specialist/Hourly_Rate

15 http://www.payscale.com/research/US/Job=Radiologist/Salary

16 http://www.payscale.com/research/US/Job=Physician_%2f_Doctor%2c_Emergency_Room_(ER)/Salary

17 Gray, K. & Herr, E. (2006). *Other Ways to Win: Creating Alternatives for High School Graduates. Third Edition.* Thousand Oaks: Corwin Press.

18 U.S. Bureau of Labor Statistics. *Occupational Outlook Handbook 2012-13.* Office of Occupational Statistics and Employment Projections.

19 Gray, K. & Herr, E. (2006). *Other Ways to Win: Creating Alternatives for High School Graduates. Third Edition.* Thousand Oaks: Corwin Press.

20 http://www.npr.org/2015/02/02/383335110/economists-say-millennials-should-consider-careers-in-trades

21 Bureau of Labor Statistics (2010). *Occupational Outlook Handbook 2010-11 Edition.* U.S. Department of Labor.

22 Department of Labor (December 8, 2010), *Table 1.3 Fastest Growing Occupations, 2008 and projected 2018.* Employment Projections Program, U.S. Bureau of Labor Statistics. Friedman, T. (2005). *The World is Flat: A Brief History of the Twenty-First Century.* New York: Farrar, Straus, and Giroux.

23 EMSI Spring 2015 occupation employment data based on Occupational Employment Statistics (QCEW and Non-QCEW Employees classes of worker) and the American Community Survey (Self-Employed and Extended Proprietors) for the State of California. Provided by the

CCC Centers of Excellence.

24 CA Employment Development Department. March 2009 baseline wage data.

25 College Measures. "Higher Education Pays: But a Lot More for Some Graduates Than For Others."

26 Dr. Mark Schneider. Assessment of STEM Higher Education. January 21, 2015. http://www.uh.edu/uh-energy/calendar/events/energy-workshop-series/assessment-of-higher-education/

27 College Measures. "Higher Education Pays: But a Lot More for Some Graduates Than For Others."

28 College Measures. "Higher Education Pays: But a Lot More for Some Graduates Than For Others."

29 College Measures. "Higher Education Pays: But a Lot More for Some Graduates Than For Others."

30 College Measures. "Higher Education Pays: But a Lot More for Some Graduates Than For Others."

31 Parnell, D. (1985). The Neglected Majority. Washington D.C.: The Community College Press.

32 http://zakslayback.com/2015/12/02/its-time-we-admit-the-degree-is-speculation-not-investment/

33 Projections of Education Statistics to 2021

34 Millennial Jobs Report, May 2015

35 Brookings Papers on Economic Activity. Fall 2015 Conference. "A crisis in student loans? How changes in the characteristics of borrowers and in the institutions they attended contributed to rising loan defaults." Adam Looney and Constantine Yannelis. http://www.brookings.edu/about/projects/bpea/papers/2015/looney-yannelis-student-loan-defaults

36 Cooperative Institutional Research Program at the Higher Education Research Institute at UCLA. "The American Freshman: National Norms Fall 2014". http://www.heri.ucla.edu/monographs/TheAmericanFreshman2014.pdf

37 http://www.epi.org/publication/the-class-of-2015/#young-college-graduates-also-face-a-tough-labor-market

38 Abel, Jaison R., and Richard Deitz. 2014. "Are the Job Prospects of Recent College Graduates Improving?" Liberty Street Economics (blog of the Federal Reserve Bank of New York), September 4. http://libertystreeteconomics.newyorkfed.org/2014/09/are-the-job-prospects-of-recent-college-graduates-improving.html#.VUt7TvlVhBc

39 http://www.aacc.nche.edu/AboutCC/Trends/Documents/completion_report_05212015.pdf

40 Community College Research Center. (2014). Community college economics for policymakers: The one big fact and the one big myth. New York, NY: Belfield, C. & Jenkins, D.

CHAPTER 6

START WITH THE END
GOAL IN MIND

What Is the Goal of Education?

"If we fail to better prepare current and future teens and young adults, their frustration over scarce and inferior opportunities is likely to grow, along with economic inequality. The quality of their lives will be lower, the costs that they impose on society will be higher, and many of their potential contributions to society will go unrealized. This is a troubling prospect for any society and almost certainly a recipe for national decline... Meanwhile, business leaders are warning that once the recession ends, they could face shortages of qualified workers in areas ranging from non-residential construction and energy to information technology, healthcare, and the STEM fields. ...almost all of these jobs require at least some post-secondary education."[1] Pathways to Prosperity, February 2011

For years, we have told high school students that in order to be successful in terms of employment, salary, and future career choices they must graduate from high school.[2] Then we have taken this a step further and said that college is also necessary. Policymakers have established a system embracing the idea that all students must be college and career ready.[3] If this is truly the goal, for students to be ready for college and career, then as educators, we must keep both these goals equally in mind when helping students determine their next steps.

To be honest with you, I take exception to the phrase 'college and career ready' because the term *college* has come to mean a 4-year university to most people. Unfortunately, technical colleges and community colleges are still too often marginalized from the "college prep" dialog. I'd love to see this idea expanded to the phrase "post-secondary education and career ready", with post-secondary education ranging from on the job training all the way through doctoral degrees. But I suppose that is not as catchy.

I would also like to see this as an "and" proposition instead of an "or" proposition. Currently, students are either prepared to attend a 4-year university OR they are prepared to enter into a career. The truth is that everyone should be prepared to enter some kind of post-secondary education AND be career ready if one of the main goals of education is truly to help students be prepared for commensurate employment.

What Is the Definition of a Good Job?

The question then becomes, "What employment?" Do we mean any employment in any sector doing anything? Or do we mean a job that can sustain a family? Or do we mean a job that the student finds meaningful? Or is it a job with advancement possibilities? Can a "good job" only exist in an office setting or can it occur anywhere? Is a "good job" one that has a 4-year degree attached to it? Is a "good job" one that doesn't require any manual labor?

In our world today, people tend to define a good job as one that makes a lot of money and requires little physical effort. In general, good jobs are white collared jobs. But you've seen that many blue collar and mid-skilled jobs are actually better in terms of monetary compensation than many more "prestigious" white collared jobs available. It seems to me that we need to redefine what it means to have a good job.

US News puts out a list of the 100 best jobs each year. According to the most recent list, all but one of the top 10 jobs requires a 4-year degree or higher.[4] Their definition of a good job is one that pays well, challenges you without stressing you out, has room for advancement, and are hiring.

But, when looking at their list, especially the top 10 jobs, you'd get the impression that the good jobs almost exclusively need a college degree. Their mix would say that only 1 in 10 could get by without a 4-year degree. Yet, in the research those numbers are nearly reversed. So, one lesson to be learned is to be a critical consumer of what you read.

In general, too many people focus on education and salary as the definition of a good job. I agree that having an income that meets your needs is desirable and even necessary. But satisfaction in your job, being able to do your job well, and feeling connected with what you do are just as important.

We need to change our conventional approaches to jobs, education, and wages. We need to focus on the needs of each student and recognize the value of skilled labor. We need to think about all of the jobs that are needed to run the world, at every level of education and experience, instead of only focusing on the smallest portion of available jobs as the goal for all.

As parents and educators, we need to be looking beyond the formal education process, whether that is a certificate, 2 year degree, 4 year degree, Masters, or even 10 years of higher education. What is the student going to do then? Is their first career in line with who they are, what they excel in, and what is available in the marketplace? Do they have the skills, not just the piece of paper, to secure employment in their field of choice? If so, who cares about the color of one's collar?

How to Choose Post-Secondary Education

In his book, *The 7 Habits of Highly Effective People*, one of Stephen Covey's seven steps is to begin with the end in mind.[5] He asks people to envision what they want in the end and then create a blueprint to get to that point. Wouldn't it be wonderful if we helped our students follow this expert advice for their own lives? But alas, this is not the way it happens. High school seniors typically determine where they want to go to school first, then they pick a major second, and then they finally pick a career. Let's examine this for a minute.

Why do seniors pick the colleges/universities they select? Perhaps their parents went there. Perhaps they love the basketball team. Perhaps their best friend has decided to go there. Maybe they want to live out of state or in a big city. While very few do, most do not pick a college because it is the right fit for what they want to accomplish in terms of education and career.

Once a student is at school, they then will typically pick a major from available options at the time. However, this often doesn't happen for a semester or two and students are labeled as "undecided" in the meantime. During this time, they take basic classes, hoping to figure out what they are interest in. Often, they decide their major based on a single class they enjoyed or because a friend wants to major in a particular field together. More often, they decide simply because the college has a policy that it is time to do so. For me, I recall sitting with the university catalog and literally crossing out majors that I didn't like, thought were hard, or didn't understand. Absent any career guidance or intentional career exploration, the process of elimination was the only way I thought to select a major.

Then finally around graduation time, students will finally pick a career and expect to get hired because they followed the one-way-to-win paradigm. Sadly, the numbers show that they are not likely to get hired, or at least not in an area related to their education.

My colleague, Teri B. Clark, describes her experience this way:

"I wanted to take a year off between high school and college because I didn't know what I wanted to be. My parents would not hear of it. I either went that year, or I was on my own. So, of course, I went.

I chose a state college because several friends were going there, and I didn't initially declare a major. I was thinking about a business degree because my mom said that I should consider running a corporation and living in some big city like Atlanta. She imagined me living in a penthouse suite. Unfortunately, I hated the business classes I took my first semester.

Eventually, I double-majored and double-minored. One major was elementary education. I chose this because there were some great scholarships available. I then majored in psychology because I really liked the classes. I minored in math because I found math courses to be easy. My final minor is the most embarrassing. It was in sociology. I had this minor because I had a crush on one of my professors. I took every class he had to offer and others in his department just so I could run into him on occasion.

I never taught in the public schools because, although I loved the idea of teaching, the reality of teaching in the public school was not something I enjoyed. I figured this out during my student teaching semester - the last semester of college. After graduation, I ended up working at a bank running checks through a scanner in the proof department. My job didn't require any of my post-secondary education at all. In fact, most of the women working in the department had no college and two hadn't graduated from high school. However, the pay scale was determined by the number of checks you could run in an hour, and I was fast. I was making more money running checks than I could as a teacher.

I became a stay-at-home mom once I got married and had small children. When they were older, I decided to become a virtual assistant. This would allow me to work at home while still being available to my children. One client asked me to write his email correspondence. He liked my writing style and asked me if I had ever written a book. Even though I had no experience, he hired me to help him write an ebook. This led to other similar opportunities, and the rest is history.

I wish that someone had talked to me about job opportunities that were available. All I knew were doctors, nurses, lawyers, teachers, business executives, and then construction type workers. None of those fit me, so I took a wide variety of classes searching for something that did. Thirteen years after graduation, I finally stumbled upon writing as a career and I love it. I try not to think of all the wasted education and all the loan debt I had to repay!"

Teri's story, as well as my own, is becoming more and more common. What should the correct order be? Should it remain selecting a college, then a major, then a career? No. When I ask seasoned adults and career guidance professionals they recommend it should be exactly the opposite. Students should first pick their initial career, determine the major or other training needed to be best positioned for that career, and then lastly research and select a school that offers what they need in terms of education and training. The career should determine the major. The major should determine the college.

The answer is to start career planning much earlier in the process. Rather than waiting until a student is a junior in college with an "-ology" major to start career planning, or even later as I did, we must help them enter into post-secondary education with an initial career goal in mind. This approach does not necessarily require any additional funding, time, or legislation. But it does require intentional guidance by a caring adult who knows how to ask the correct questions.

1 Pathways to Prosperity, February 2011 http://www.gse.harvard.edu/sites/default/files//documents/Pathways_to_Prosperity_Feb2011-1.pdf
2 Gwynne, J., Lesnick, J., Hart, H., & Allensworth, E. (2009). What Matters for Staying On-Track and Graduating in
Chicago Public Schools: A Focus on Students with Disabilities
3 Pinkus, Lindsay (2009). Action Required: Addressing the Nation's Lowest-Performing High Schools. Washington,
D.C.: Alliance for Excellent Education. Retrieved April 7, 2010, from http://www.all4ed.org/files/ActionRequired.pdf.
4 http://money.usnews.com/careers/best-jobs/rankings/the-100-best-jobs#
5 The 7 Habits of Highly Effective People: Powerful Lessons in Personal Change. Stephen Covery. 1990.

CHAPTER 7

ADDING "R"S: MAKING SENSE OF MODERN EDUCATION

Reading – wRiting – aRithmetic

Everyone has heard of the three R's – Reading, writing, and arithmetic. Of course, for good spellers, calling these three R's doesn't make a lot of sense; it's really an R, W, and an A! Nonetheless, for generations, we have focused on these three Rs as a foundation for all our students regardless of their educational direction. A blind focus on these three in a cookie-cutter fashion has eventually led us to the one-way-to-win philosophy. Learn to read, learn to write, and learn how to do math, and then head on to college to do... anything.

I have learned from countless industry partners that these three are still important, but they need to be contextualized. Treating all students the same in these subject areas is no longer working. We know that thousands of students each year quit high school or never complete their college because they just don't see the point to the educational process. With high unemployment rates for 4-year graduates, it is no wonder that so many throw in the towel.

I believe that these 3 R's are needed, but are alone inadequate. My recommendation is that we add two more Rs to make education fit today's goal of preparing all students to be career ready.

Relevance

The fourth R should be relevance. Too many students are asking, "Why do I need to learn this?" I asked my high school math teacher this very question when learning about the Pythagorean Theorem. He had it up on the board and was explaining that it was the relationship among the three sides of a right triangle. You may recall from high school that the square of the hypotenuse is equal to the sum of the squares of the other two sides.

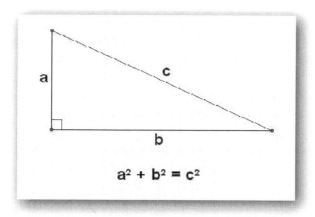

$$a^2 + b^2 = c^2$$

I asked my teacher why I would ever need to know this and he gave me the wisdom that so many teachers give students: "Trust me. You'll need it someday." Well, to this day I have not used this theorem in my professional nor personal life. Have you?

Research shows, and I believe, it is important for students to understand the relevance of what they are learning. For instance, if I had gone into engineering or construction, I undoubtedly would have used this equation. In fact, most math and geometry classes do have relevance if you are going into an engineering or math-related field.

Does this mean that only those going into a math related field need to learn it? No, of course not. But showing a student how figuring out real-world construction problems with the Pythagorean Theorem would certainly give context to the math being learned. Now, instead of some abstract theorem, they have a hands-on understanding of its use.

In general, if students do not know why something is important to them or how it will affect their ultimate career, it won't matter very much. Giving them platitudes like "trust me" or "you'll find out when you're older" only increases the high school dropout rate. Recall from chapter two that the main reasons students drop out are due to a lack or relevancy, boredom, or no perceived career-applicability.

The Bill and Melinda Gates Foundation did a study a few years ago on high school dropouts. I found this a particularly fascinating population to survey. They found that over 74% of dropouts had passing grades. When asked why they quit, they said that they didn't feel that what they were learning was relevant to them. They had career ideas in mind but no one was discussing with them how what they were learning in English class would pertain to their end goal.

This about it this way: Have you ever been quoted out of context? Well, I think we've been teaching out of context for too long...isolating knowledge separate from its application and real-world relevancy.

To truly ensure subjects have relevance to one's future career, students will need to go through self-exploration and then career exploration first. Then, as they learn, they will be able to see why the content they are presenting in their classes matter. The trick to increasing internal motivation is to help students see how the content is applicable to their initial career choice.

Reality

The fifth R should be Reality. What is really out there in the job market today? How does one really seek out a career? What are employers really looking for in an employee? What skills are really necessary to find a good job?

The reality is that a piece of paper stating you have a 4-year degree is no longer sufficient in getting people a job because it does not automatically mean you have the right skills for the labor market. Being well-educated is not the same thing as being employable. Read this sentence again and think about what it means: Being well-educated is not the same thing as being employable.

Of course, no educator or counselor is going to be able to know the reality of all job markets. Thankfully, we have many systems that can help us know what is going on locally, nationally, and globally. We simply need to know where the resources are and be able to direct students appropriately whether they want to be an author or a zoologist or anything in between.

Recently, a local community college in California released a list of all their students that had declared a two-year transfer degree. That list showed that 202 students were attempting to earn their degree in sociology and planning to transfer to a 4-year institution to get their bachelor's in sociology.

So, I went to monster.com and put in the local zip code with a 50-mile radius of that college, which happens to cover an area with approximately 30 other community colleges. I put in the keyword "sociology" to pop up anywhere in the job description, in any industry, where the knowledge, experience, and/or theories of sociology would be helpful to that employee. Just 16 available jobs popped up on that given day.

That means 202 students will be competing for 16 jobs. But it gets worse. Remember, there were 30 other community colleges in the area, each likely with another 200 sociology majors. That's approximately 6,000 sociology majors competing for 16 jobs. Now, even accounting for all the other types of occupations a student could secure with a sociology degree (counselor, rehabilitation, therapist, case worker, social worker, etc.), my revised and expanded job search resulted with only 91 job postings.

Do the 6,000 students pursuing a sociology degree know the competition they will be facing? If they do and still want to get a sociology degree then that is great. They should go for it, and I support their informed decision 100 percent. But if they are doing it thinking they will make a six-figure income when they graduate because they just need a degree in anything, then the fifth R – Reality – is not being used.

In 2014, I put together a short animated video called *Success in the New Economy* outlining the concepts that eventually evolved into this book. [1] Initially I thought that only fifteen people and my mother would watch the video. But, with over 1 million viewers within its first year I have been surprised and humbled with the warm reception it has received. One parent recently wrote to thank me for the paradigm-shift she experienced while watching the video. Her comments really emphasize the need for these additional two R's:

"I want to take a moment to thank you for your video titled 'Success in the New Economy.'" I am a parent of a bright high school senior. However, evaluating his intelligence by his GPA would cause you to doubt my last statement. If a teacher lacks the ability to connect and interest him, he doesn't see the point in showing them just how able he is. This, as you might imagine, has added to the typical teen-parent relationship stress in our household.

As parents, his dad and I have struggled for several years trying to impress upon him the value of good grades and a 4-year college education. Yet, at the same time, we know that the degrees that we earned in 1983 haven't necessarily helped propel us farther than many of our peers, or even younger colleagues. Over the last few years, our beliefs have shifted somewhat toward what your video describes, but until watching your video several times, I couldn't unclench from my fist the long-held beliefs that our son has to go to a 4-year university, even if he doesn't know what he wants to 'be/do' after that.

It is a big relief around our household now to be letting go of how we thought things should be. I am now feeling excited to support my son with his plan to research a few local technical colleges!"

If you haven't seen the *Success in the New Economy* video, I encourage you to look it up and view it now. It is hosted on www.vimeo.com and is also linked from my website www.TelosES.com. Let me know what you think!

Reality in Action in California

As previously mentioned, technical skills are the new currency in today's world and the majority of positions that pay good wages require skills associated with at least some education beyond high school.[2] A good number of high-skilled, family-supporting occupations are known as "middle-skilled jobs," which require more than a high school education but less than a four-year degree. In fact, middle-skill jobs represent the largest share of jobs in California - some 49 percent - and they are the largest share of future job openings.[3] Despite these numbers, which are similar throughout the United States, the reality is that most students are not getting the training they need for the jobs that are available.[4] This is where you can provide real value to your students as they begin to explore options available to them after high school.

The research says that "about half of all jobs are classified as middle-skill, but only 38 percent of California workers have the education and training required to fill these positions." Wow! In reality, this skill gap is likely even greater in certain industries because many workers trained to the middle-skill level, and even those with bachelor's degrees, did not have the specific technical skills needed when they entered the workforce and were trained on the job. This means that thousands of well-paid and rewarding jobs are going unfilled in California, and every other state, and many are in industries that are essential to our nation's economy.[5]

Reality Check: High skilled entry-level and technician jobs today require individuals that have a wide range of knowledge, skills, and problem solving ability that the average high schools simply do not provide.[6]

Reality of Middle-Skill Jobs

According to the Department of Labor, of the thirty fastest growing occupations between 2008-2018, all will require some education beyond high school (for example, home health aides, biomedical engineers, dental hygienists, pharmacy technicians, and environmental engineer technicians).[7] But only 14 of the 30 will require education at, or beyond, a 4-year baccalaureate degree. The other sixteen of the fastest growing 30 jobs in America will require career & technical education (CTE). That typically means either a technical certificate beyond high school or a 2-year Associate's Degree.

So, by pushing the "college for all" agenda, we have managed to produce many high school dropouts without skills, many high school graduates without skills, many college dropouts without skills, and many college graduates without skills, all while the labor market is screaming for highly-trained skilled technicians. You see, to many employers, one's diploma often serves as little more than proof of attendance.[8]

Relevance and Reality: College-Prep and Career-Prep are Complementary

Fortunately, we know how to reduce this skills gap and ensure our educational system better aligns with employer expectations in order for individual students to be successful. All we need to do is re-learn that college-prep and career and technical education (CTE) are complementary and not competing goals.

Research shows that CTE keeps high school students engaged while producing higher attendance rates, lower dropout rates, higher graduation rates, and increased completion of college preparatory courses.[9] In fact, a combination of 60% academic courses and 40% CTE is the most effective drop-out prevention program in the American high school.[10]

We know that CTE students are more likely than others to earn a certificate, 2-year degree, get and keep a job, or transfer to a 4-year university.[11] We also know that CTE students not only attend college in higher numbers than non-CTE students, but they receive promotions and pay increases at higher rates than students that did not take technical courses.[12]

Taking advantage of career and technical education courses seems to be the only true way to prepare students for both for college and career! Some districts have figured this out and have even required at least one CTE course for high school graduation. Others, such as the State of North Carolina (detailed in chapter three), have created an equal option for high school graduation which emphasizes CTE courses.

There are many ways for your student to earn a great living and be successful and most of these paths require mastering technical skills. Rather than blindly advocating bachelor's degrees as the golden passport to financial abundance to your students, it may be wise to place our advice in context of the labor market, and promote with equal tenacity career and technical education in order to ensure the majority of our youth are not unprepared for the transition to the workforce.

Bringing CTE Back

Prior to the 1950's, the three Rs were taught alongside vocational education classes. Most adults remember industrial arts classes where they learned about wood working and metal working. Hands-on projects were a part of the school day. This all changed when educators decided that those with the ability to go to college didn't need shop class but needed additional science and foreign language classes instead. Only those students with a "lower ability" and not going to college would take anything resembling vocational education.

Eventually, parents and educators rejected the "track by ability" idea, saying that those who were poor or from ethnic descent were not getting equal chances to go to college. Since non-college bound students were taking vocational education, it began to be seen as the remedial track; e.g. the classes you took if you weren't bright enough for the better plan known as college.

Even when tracking was eliminated, vocational education remained the ugly step-child. The focus shifted to 'college for all' and the high school curriculum reflected this through the removal of most vocational education opportunities. In fact, today, even though four-year university grads are increasingly unemployable, states continue to cut funding to vocational and technical skill-building programs.

You may be wondering why CTE classes are the first to go. Elected officials and administrators always point to the cost of operation. But when we realize that most students do not go to college and need these skills, are CTE classes really expendable? No! Instead, this should be the thrust of our educational movement because technical ability is where many jobs of the future will be.

And this brings us right back to the two additional Rs: relevancy and reality. CTE classes are the most relevant to students today as high schools and colleges seek to get students ready for a career. CTE classes are also part of the reality of the 21st century economy. A majority of the jobs available in the labor market require less than a 4-year degree. Today's students need the skills being taught in CTE classes, combined with a strong general education foundation, to secure the good jobs of tomorrow and to become working members of our society.

It's time for our educational system to stop focusing on just the 3 Rs and the college-prep path, which is usually interpreted as university-for-all. If we focus on content relevance and the labor market reality, in addition to the 3 Rs, our students will be more prepared to succeed.

---

1 www.TelosES.com. *Success in the New Economy* is also available in high definition at www. Vimeo.com

2 Carnevale, A., & Derochers, D. (2003). *Standards for what? The economic roots of K-16 reform.* Princeton, NJ: Educational Testing Service.

3 The Workforce Alliance. (2009). *California's Forgotten Middle-Skill Jobs: Meeting the Demands of a 21st Century Economy.* Washington DC.

4 Symonds, W., Schwartz, R., & Ferguson, R. (February 2011). *Pathways to Prosperity: Meeting the Challenge of Preparing Young Americans for the 21st Century.* Report issued by the Pathways to Prosperity Project, Harvard Graduate School of Education.

5 The Workforce Alliance. (2009). *California's Forgotten Middle-Skill Jobs: Meeting the Demands of a 21st Century Economy.* Washington DC.

6 Scott, J., and Sarkees-Wircenski, M. (2004). *Overview of Career and Technical Education: Third Edition*. Homewood, Illinois: American Technical Publishers, Inc.

7 Department of Labor (December 8, 2010), *Table 1.3 Fastest Growing Occupations, 2008 and projected 2018*. Employment Projections Program, U.S. Bureau of Labor Statistics.

8 Achieve, Inc. (2004). *Ready or Not: Creating a High School Diploma That Counts*. The American Diploma Project.

9 Castellano, M., Stringfield, S., & Stone III, J.R. (2003). Secondary career and technical education and comprehensive school reform: Implications for research and practice. *Review of Educational Research*, 73, 231-272. And: Cohen & Besharov (2004) The important role of career & technical education: Implications for federal policy [*Welfare Reform Academy Report*]. Washington DC: American Enterprise Institute for Public Policy Research. And: Brown, C. H. (2000). "A Comparison of Selected Outcomes of Secondary Tech Prep Participants and Non-Participants in Texas." *Journal of Vocational Education Research*, 25, no. 3, 273-295. And: Cardon, P. L. (Winter-Spring 2000). "At-Risk Students and Technology Education: A Qualitative Study." *Journal of Technology Studies*, 26, no. 1, 49-57.

10 Plank, DeLuca & Estacion (2008). High school dropout and the role of CTE: A survival analysis of surviving high school. *Sociology of Education*, 81, 345-370.

11 Harvey, M. W. (Spring 2001). "The Efficacy of Vocational Education for Students with Disabilities Concerning Post-School Employment Outcomes: A Review of the Literature." *Journal of Industrial Teacher Education* 38, no. 3: 25-44.

12 Adler, L. (2010). *California Career & Technical Education 2010 Longitudinal Study*, University of California, Riverside; School Improvement Research Group. And: Mitchell, D. (2006). *California Regional Occupational Centers and Programs 2006 Longitudinal Study*. University of California, Riverside; School Improvement Research Group.

CHAPTER 8

BEING PART OF THE SOLUTION

No matter where in the educational field you find yourself, as a parent, teacher, or administrator, you need to be concerned about CTE programs. All students, those that are 4-year university-bound and those that are seeking certificates and 2-year degrees, all need CTE classes in order to be gainfully employed after their post-secondary education and training.

I've been talking to educators about this issue for over ten years. I've heard all the complaints. I know that there isn't enough money in the budget for the CTE programs. I recognize that CTE programs are marginalized. The state requirements, testing mandates, metrics and external demands from parents and board members are overwhelming. I really do understand that needed skills and required classes aren't aligned. I know CTE programs are understaffed. I recognized institutions don't have enough room, priority, visibility, or attention highlighted on CTE programs. But, to be honest, although many have merit, I'm pretty tired of hearing the complaints isolated from possible solutions.

As parents and educators we understand the need to fix problems rather than simply complaining about them. It is time to stop the water-cooler venting and actually take small steps in the right direction to change the situation. Passionate leaders not only identify a problem, but they solve it. They create action plans, galvanize support, inform the masses, and move progress forward. Are you willing to be part of the solution?

If so, I have identified 17 action steps that we can focus on right now that will help all students, regardless of their initial educational pathway. My challenge to you is to not only read these recommendations, but commit to implementing at least two of these ideas in your own home/ school/community/state.

When I told a colleague I was going to include a chapter with tangible solutions to help reduce underemployment and unemployment while changing the paradigm we have of career and technical education, she chuckled. Then she quipped, "If you could help keep more kids in school and reduce the skills gap, districts will build statues of you and name schools after you across the country." So, here is my stab at immortality, in no particular order:

1. (Re)Define Counseling

Policy makers and educational leaders make big assumptions about guidance counseling. They are under the impression that a guidance counselor guides the students towards careers as well as academia. The truth, however, is that most guidance counselors (i.e. school counselors) have morphed into strictly academic counselors.

Typically, a counselor has only 30 to 45 minutes with a student per year. The main questions asked by high school counselors are, "What college do you plan to attend," and/or "What will your major be in college?" Similarly, the main question a college counselor initially asks is "What is your major?" The rest of the time is typically spent on charting classes that need to be taken to fulfill the requirements for graduation or the identified major. This may be called general counseling, guidance counseling, or school counseling...but really what is occurring is academic counseling.

Conversely, career counseling consists of talking about skills, interests, and aspirations in relation to the labor market and specific industries/occupations. If you are really counseling a student on their career, then you get to know them and understand how to best leverage their abilities and goals towards a fulfilling career. You guide them to understand themselves first.

If you are a school counselor, but find yourself only doing academic counseling, be sure to use the words "academic counseling" when describing your position. Helping others outside the profession (including elected officials that control your budget) understand this subtle but important difference in terminology and function can create the opportunity to offer more resources for career guidance. If you are a guidance counselor proactively infusing true self-exploration and career counseling into your sessions, promote what you do as a career counselor and how you do it...many tell me you are rare; you are deeply appreciated.

If we can refine our terminology and differentiate between the 'academic' and 'career' types of counseling functions, I believe we will begin to highlight what is actually occurring compared to what is actually needed.

2. Create Parallel Paths to High School Graduation

Oftentimes, our public educational systems are very well intentioned but misguided. As a result, many high school graduation standards exist to move students into college. For years, some CTE teachers have railed against these standards, especially when these college-prep graduation standards become difficult to meet for those not intending to go on to a 4-year degree. The problem is that being anti-standards (or being perceived as such) doesn't help anybody. Instead of being vocal against the standards, suggest alternatives... not because the current standards are bad or wrong, but because they are simply insufficient.

CTE classes, and CTE student organizations, give students the opportunity to look at a wide range of subjects from creative to technical, which provide specific learning goals. Such classes may include those in construction, welding, firefighting, crime scene investigation, culinary arts, anatomy and physiology, nursing, veterinary science, computer software, graphic arts, mechanical engineering, architectural drafting, business, hospitality management, and marketing (just to name a few). Students taking these classes walk away with skills needed for life that comes after high school. Since that is the case, these classes need to be part of every student's education.

Help your school system see that there need to be substitutions for graduation requirements. Let's create parallel, not alternative, paths... this AND that. For instance, perhaps a CTE class in veterinary science could be used instead of chemistry, or a class in architectural drawing could be used to meet a graduation requirement instead of a higher level math course. If you suggest alternatives rather than just being against the current system, you will help those creating the pathways to graduation to see the need for CTE classes. This approach helps all students.

Commit to sharing that if we want students to succeed, we need to prepare them for further education AND the world of work. The world of work no longer requires students to get a 4-year degree in anything. Instead, and/or in addition, all students need to obtain skills that will prepare them for careers.

Claremont Unified School District in Southern California, and many others nationally, have taken symbolic steps in requiring one CTE class for high school graduation with great success. The State of North Carolina is also an exemplar offering two equal options for high school graduation requirements, one of which emphasizes CTE. Additionally, with over 10,000 CTE courses meeting "A-G" university entrance requirements in California, there is a strong argument to be made that CTE courses can be the best of both worlds.[1]

Studies have shown that students that take CTE classes in high school are more likely to graduate,[2] more likely to complete post-secondary training,[3] and more likely to find employment at the end of their education.[4] Additionally, CTE students develop better problem-solving, project completion, research, math, college application, work-related, communication, time management, and critical-thinking skills during high school than those that did not take CTE classes.[5]

With such great rewards for students and for businesses, it makes sense to alter graduation requirements to include at least one CTE class either as a requirement or at least as an option which "counts" to help all students gain the technical skills they will need in the workforce.

3. Go to One Board Meeting a Year – Just One!

What is in the news when it comes to schools and how they are doing? End of year test scores, SAT scores, AP exams, and the number of students accepted into college. What is not in the news? Just about anything to do with CTE. So, when the talk turns to budgeting, CTE is not at the forefront of anyone's mind.

I know that you are busy. Trust me, I get it. In fact, I know that educators work long hours with very little recognition, and involved parents barely have 3 minutes to rub together at the end of the day. But part of the reason CTE is marginalized is because no one is in the room driving the conversation towards CTE. If you aren't there to remind them that CTE exists, they won't think of career planning or technical skill acquisition when it comes time for allotting funds to needed programs.

One way to change this is to go to one board meeting every year. Just one! Share the successes of your CTE students. Educate the elected officials on the numbers of students that need career and technical education classes. Let them know about the number of jobs in your area that require some kind of technical skill. Even if you are an educator that has little to do with CTE programs, you certainly understand their value. It is up to you to help others see that value, too.

If you are a CTE educator, share what is changing your field of expertise. Talk about an industry tour you recently took. Highlight a student who recently secured gainful employment because of your program. Don't attend the meeting to ask for anything nor to complain – simply go and speak with a goal of reminding them that CTE exists, is working, and is necessary. Thank them for their continued support. Invite them to your next industry advisory meeting or student showcase event. In fact, bring your students with you to the board meeting to share, demonstrate, display, and promote their projects from class. Create a dialog where none existed before.

Can you imagine the shift in the larger dialog if every educator and parent you know attended just one board meeting a year to promote career readiness and CTE? There would be a line at every podium in every board meeting all focused on discussing the value and vitality of career and technical education. Wow!

4. Calculate Your 9th Graders

One thing you could share with your board members as well as your administration would be the actual funnel for ninth graders in your school or district. Chapter 2 discusses the number of students that start in the ninth grade in California versus the number that graduate with a 4-year university degree and become gainfully employed in their field securing a living wage. Consider doing the same thing for your specific region/ state. Do it yourself or team up with your district/county researcher to compile the data.

The visual of seeing just how many students start out in the school system and how many "win" using the university-for-all model can be very enlightening. Calculate it with integrity, and then share the data widely. Offer suggestions for improving the odds for all students. They'll be listening.

5. Legislative Advocacy: Promote Apprenticeships

South Carolina has begun a program that is simple and effective. Apprenticeship Carolina offers businesses a $1,000 tax incentive for accepting apprentices in their place of business. [6] The businesses only need to fill out a one-page form that states how many apprentices they have and then they multiply that number by $1,000. [7]

We know that combining relevant education with job experience helps create success when it comes time to go to work. Job experiences through apprenticeships give students the opportunity to learn while earning income. South Carolina states on their website that, "This forward-focused program works to ensure a well-educated, well-trained workforce for South Carolina's continued competitiveness in attracting and retaining business and industry." [8]

In addition to helping students learn skills, employers benefit as well. Apprenticeship programs create a pipeline of future employees, reduce turnover rates, and teach skills specifically needed by their company, all while earning a tax credit. This is a win-win for everyone.

We know that if you incentivize something, more of that something happens. This is true in South Carolina where apprenticeships are popping up in places like legal offices and psychiatric hospitals in addition to the traditional skilled trades. In 2007, there were only 90 registered apprenticeship programs in South Carolina. Today, there are 768 apprenticeship programs helping 6,453 students gain valuable skills a year.[9] One piece of policy has changed the economy, the focus/relevancy of a child's education, and the entire educational system in the state.

Find out whether or not programs like Apprenticeship Carolina exist in your state. Write a letter to your legislator and invite them to your school. Be sure to include the benefits CTE courses provide to students and for the state's economy. Look over the South Carolina program and watch the testimonials. Explain how easy it is for companies to participate and explain why its simplicity is crucial.

In addition to writing a letter, consider talking with a state legislator in person. The more they hear about the need for CTE training and the successes of other states, the more likely they are to consider a similar program. Don't wait for weeks to speak to your locally elected official themselves. Scheduling a meeting to chat with their staff can be equally as effective. Build a relationship with them.

If you happen to live in a state where a viable apprenticeship or CTE program is working, write a letter of support stating why you are happy with the program. CTE programs are often put on the chopping block when economic times are tough, despite that being the time when CTE programs are most necessary. If legislators hear good things about the program when economic times are good, they are less likely to cut it when the budget constricts.

6. Embed Career Exploration into Curriculum

Many people think of career exploration as a separate entity or class. Although having a separate class is fine, it is also possible, and may be preferable, to explore careers while learning in the current curriculum. Many biology classes contain a lesson plan on viruses. While studying the viruses, students in some schools learn about different careers associated with studying viruses such as pathologists, virologists, vaccine development, research associate, lab technician, grant writer, product development, laboratory information systems, database systems, and forensics to name a few.

After Biology comes English class in which the student writes about the education needed for one of the many careers available in a laboratory setting. During math class, the teacher points out how the math being taught is actively used in conducting vaccine and medical research.

When we embed curriculum strategies, and overtly discuss career exploration in core classes, it helps students link their learning to future careers. This helps students discover their interests as well as explore pathways to get those careers. All students need to have an understanding of what is out there in the labor market. By infusing career exploration into every course, or within learning communities where the faculty from different courses speak and coordinate their content, a student can begin to see not only what is available to them but also the interdisciplinary connection of knowledge. This can even be achieved without changing any of the current curriculum standards.

For example, the Ohio Department of Education has started what they call Career Connections.[10] They feel that every child should understand the connection between what they are learning in school and the career they eventually choose. To do this, they have created an embedded curriculum that begins as early as kindergarten and gets more specific as the students move into high school.

One example shared by the department is embedding career exploration and skills attainment into a language arts class:

> Students will brainstorm characteristics of effective speakers and look for them as they watch selected video clips. After viewing videos of three dynamic speakers, students will talk about how communications skills are important across all types of jobs (for example, hospitality, IT or health). Students will include communication skills in their plans for education and training through high school and beyond.[11]

Another available resource for embedding career exploration comes from the California Career Resource Network (CalCRN) program from the California Department of Education. They have created an easy to use set of lessons that can be used in grade 5 through 12 to help expose students to the many facets of becoming career ready. The Career and College Readiness Lesson Plans can be used by anyone nationwide. They can be found on the CalCRN Web site at www.californiacareers.info.

We know most jobs will require some kind of training beyond high school. By embedding career exploration into the curriculum, we will have the opportunity to help students discover what excites them and what they need to do to take on a particular profession. We will be able to make the link for students between what they are learning and their future career.

Does every teacher and administrator in your district have the tools and knowledge to help students explore careers? Do they each see themselves as being a career coach? If not, embedding career exploration into existing curriculum/programs is a relatively inexpensive and very powerful place to start.

7. Learn About Micro-Credentials

If you have ever known a scout, you have seen the idea of a micro-credential, also known as a merit badge. These physical badges allow others to see what you have learned. Digital badges are similar but are used to allow digital users to see what you have accomplished. Essentially, digital badges are merit-badge-like qualifications that certify that the bearer of the badge has learned a particular skill or set of skills.

In 2011, a white paper by Peer 2 Peer University and the Mozilla Foundation got educators interested in the idea of using badges to certify that students had accomplished specific learning modules in a game-like atmosphere.[12] One badge system currently in use is Pluralsight. This system tests users on over 500 subjects on things such as Photoshop, PowerPoint, Java, accounting, and more. While there are many platforms and options, the concept is quite impactful.

The badges earned allows others know what students have achieved and also allows the user to know what more they need to learn to improve.

Digital badges can help contribute to the gamification of education and would be a great addition to classroom learning. Rather than having a grade in an English class that only tells a college or employer that they completed the course with a specific grade, badges would tell which skills they completed, such as technical writing or APA format usage. Now, instead of a letter grade, students would be able to show the actual skills they've mastered. These badges are often displayed on social media sites as well as on posted resumes or in an electronic portfolio.

Essentially, these badges break down mountains of competencies into smaller skill sets. If this were done well, a student could earn certain skill sets to attain a degree rather than take certain courses. So, if someone needed certain geometry skills for a construction trade, those skills would be listed and the student would only need to take the sections related to their certificate or degree choice.

How might this approach help students? First of all, as this idea expands it will give students the ability to identity and gain specific skills. Cisco and A+ certifications are already more valuable than an AS in computer science for some jobs. Having badges/credentials that let employers know what the potential employee can do is often more beneficial than a diploma that doesn't directly explain competencies.

This approach may also help create alternate routes to a 4-year degree. Organizations can now say that having specific badges are needed to apply and these competencies don't all have to come from educational organizations.

Finally, badges and micro-credentials will help with the idea of personalized learning that fits the needs and strengths of each individual student. A student with an interest in a given field will be able to gain a collection of badges to represent their actual skills, essentially creating a digital transcript about their strengths and real-world abilities.

8. Promote Dual/Concurrent Enrollment and Articulation Equal to AP Classes

As aforementioned, Advanced Placement (AP) courses are high school classes offered at a college level. When the class is completed, students can take a test to determine if they will receive college credit. If a college accepts AP tests and a student passes with a certain score, then the student gets credit for taking this class and does not need to repeat the class in college.

AP classes have been around a while and they have a strong following. The problem is that of the 1.5 million students that actually take the test, just more than 1 in 8 passes with a score of 3 or better (out of a 5-point scale).[13] Luckily, there are alternatives to the AP class with much better odds of getting ahead in college. These include concurrent enrollment, dual enrollment, and articulated classes.

Concurrent enrollment is when school students are enrolled in community college coursework while still in high school, and the courses are approved by both the community college and high school district. However, the courses are typically offered on a community college campus (or at the high school). High school students are held to the same standards as other college students, plus they may have to pay some college fees (including a health fee and the cost of textbooks) depending on your state's policy.

Dual enrollment is when a high school student is enrolled in a community college course at their high school during the traditional school day. The courses are approved by both the community college and high school district just as with concurrent enrollment. The courses are usually offered on the high school campus and taught by high school faculty who meet community college minimum qualifications.

Finally, there is articulation. This process involves the development of course-to-course articulation agreements developed between high school and community college faculty when the two parties agree that the high school and community college course are equivalent. Students earn college credit when they earn a passing grade in their aligned high school course (the grade is sometimes specified). Depending on the district, credit will either be granted immediately or when they apply to the college upon showing their high school transcript.

So, let's look at the data. Only about 13% of students taking an AP class will get college credit. For those taking an articulated class, 91% get the college credit. For those that completed a dual or concurrent enrollment class, 100% got the college credit. It would seem to me that we should be encouraging these more successful options instead of just Advanced Placement.

9. Measure What Matters

Let's begin by thinking about buying a TV. Prior to buying a TV, we learn about the features that make a TV good or bad. Most shoppers look at the screen size first. Then they move on to things such as HD vs Ultra HD vs OLED. Those "in the know" suggest that the best resolution is above 1080 pixels and that the refresh rate needs to be at least 120 Hz. If you do this, you are bound to get a decent TV. However, there are questions we don't ask. For instance, no one cares how much it weighs because the weight of the TV has nothing at all to do with the quality of the picture. But the weight is data that is readily available, is it not?

What are the metrics that matter in education? The first is how many students graduate and can be employed? How many actually complete college? Like the weight of the TV, some things we measure just don't matter. For instance, how many students go straight to college? Why doesn't this matter? Because the number doesn't look at how many make it through to the end. Getting only a year or two in a 4-year degree at a university can be a significant waste of time and money.

Take for example the Academic Performance Index (API) score in California which is a measurement of academic performance and process of individual schools. The API is a number between 200 and 1000 that reflects a school's performance level based on assessments. These assessments include the California Standards Tests (CST), California Modified Assessment (CMA), California Alternative Performance Assessment (CAPA), and California High School Exit Examination (CAHSEE). Each of these tests focuses on a combination of English, math, history, and/or science. Not one CTE assessment is used to create this score. Career exploration has not historically been a variable in determining the quality of a school. How many students eventually graduate from post-secondary education with any certificate/degree is also not a factor, nor is how many students secure employment at a living wage. In many respects, a school's API score is analogous to the weight of a television set: easy to measure, but not a true indicator of quality. A task force has been formed to look at developing a new accountability system to change/augment the API score, but their recommendations have not been released at the time of this book's publishing.[14]

We need to be looking at the data that show a real picture of what is happening in education. If we honestly assess education to show not just university-bound goals, but also other post-secondary education goals, we will be able to determine if our schools are truly succeeding at helping students find a good job and secure a rewarding career. We need to be sure that we are measuring what really matters and not measuring out of convenience.

10. Discuss Ways to Develop Skill Mastery vs. Seat Time

The point of taking a class is to master the material involved. Over time, educators began equating mastery with the amount of time spent learning, rather than the actual mastery of concepts.

The idea of "butts in the seat" or the Carnegie unit was originally created to calculate the pensions of faculty. Eventually, the Carnegie unit became the standard to determine how many credits a person received for taking a class. Instead of a student learning what needs to be learned and moving on, they are either forced to sit in a chair after learning a topic or forced to move on before a topic is understood.

Wouldn't it be great if we could focus on mastery again? Policy makers, industries, and universities have begun to challenge the standard models of learning and credentialing. Rather than stress exposure to material, this idea stresses mastery of a concept. This is known as competency-based learning and has no time-frame, nor does it have to be accomplished in a traditional classroom. Another is called stackability. This suggests that not every student will take the same path at the same pace, even when they are working towards the same degree.

A paper prepared for the American Council on Education's Center for Education Attainment and Innovation calls for a new post-secondary education credentialing system, which would provide tangible benefits for students, workers, and employers. The authors write, "A less confusing, high-quality system of portable, stackable credentials is a matter of equity for individuals of all skill levels seeking to climb the economic ladder and a matter of economic competitiveness for the nation as it seeks to increase workforce capacity and productivity."[15]

One way to do this would be to base classes on the content that is being taught and learned rather than on the year one was born. If a student needs a class in fractions, they go take it, no matter their chronological age. When they have mastered that skill/content, they could then move on to another class immediately.

Another somewhat controversial idea would be to completely flip school. The "flipped classroom" model is not new, but many teachers and faculty members have not yet tried/embraced this proven model. Using this method, students watch a prerecorded lecture while at home instead of in class. In this way, the best of the best teachers could offer lectures on a multitude of topics. Perhaps even the Teacher of the Year from another state would deliver the best lecture to every child via the internet. Then, the student heads into school and applies what they learned from the lecture in laboratories, simulations, and hands-on activities. Local teachers could then become learning facilitators and coaches; able to go deeper with the course content helping students to apply it to hand-on scenarios and real world problems.

You may think this is a pie in the sky idea, but Clintondale High School in Clinton, Michigan is trying something very similar. Students spend their school time working on projects and assignments. Their homework is watching the lessons via video and audio. The best part is that it is working. Since it was implemented in 2010, the graduation rate has increased to almost 100%, and the failure rates for English and Math have been reduced by 33% and 31% respectively.[16] Wow!!

11. Co-Locate State Career Centers and Schools

This is a recommendation primarily for our technical and community colleges, though high schools students should have some basic knowledge about regional career center resources. All states have some kind of job placement or career assistance center funded by the government to help those that are unemployed find a job and/or get additional training. Called either One Stop Centers, American Career Centers, Workforce Investment Board Centers, America's Job Centers, etc., these county-led agencies provide workshops, financial education/training assistance, case management, and help connect residents to jobs. Many community and technical colleges have similar centers on each campus working with students connecting them with internships, workshops, and employment with local employers.

This function should be happening together. There is no need to have career centers operated by the unemployment office and the college doing the same thing but on different sites. I fear we are duplicating efforts and not leveraging the expertise, connections, and resources from two parallel systems. Instead, let's consider the merits of focusing our efforts on the college campus where training can easily occur. Stop the redundancy. Let's co-locate government sponsored career and training centers at our technical and community colleges.

12. Align School Budgets with Labor Market Needs

I have to admit that this is a pipe dream, but it is definitely worth a conversation with those creating the budgets for our school systems. The premise is that we are currently misaligned. Much of the budget is going towards making students university ready when evidence suggests that more middle-skill job training is needed.

The goal would be that if the local/state economy needs 64% of the labor market with CTE skills, then 64% of the budget should go towards CTE programs and contextualized classes. The budgets would fluctuate yearly depending on the state or regional needs. Of course, this isn't going to happen, but putting the idea out there will help others look at

CTE and employability-preparation needs versus the current budgeting process. At the very minimum, I think it would be an interesting conversation starter to calculate the percentage of your district's current budget directed to CTE and career preparation compared to your local labor market demands.

13. Flip the College Decision-Making Paradigm

It's quite shocking when you think about it. Ask any adult to describe how they approached three significant life choices – their major, their college, and their career. Ask them to recall, in order, which they chose first, second and third.

They'll probably tell you that the first thing they chose was the college they wanted to attend. Perhaps they picked a parent's alma mater, or one based upon location. And after choosing a college, most settled next on their major, but usually not right away. And that choice is too often driven by current interests or the persuasion from a friend to declare the same major.

Finally, somewhere near or even after graduation, they then picked their career. They embarked onto the job to market expecting to get hired given their education. But in today's economy that is a rude awakening for students and parents alike. Thirty-three percent of college graduates are still underemployed well into their thirties.[17]

As discussed in chapter six, most graduating high school students today make these choices in the same order. But when we ask self-aware, mature adults what the selection order should be, they respond without hesitation; choose an initial career first, a college major second, and the college itself third. This order just makes sense. Your career choice dictates what major to pursue, which in turn helps identify the best college choice.

Our educational system is very well-intentioned, but incredibly misaligned. The truth is, the pendulum has swung too far toward college preparation and away from career preparation.

We encourage a college-going-culture even as early as elementary school with university pendants decorating 2nd grade classrooms. And an exorbitant amount of time in high school is spent on college application essays and financial aid applications. At some point in recent history we have transitioned from asking the more important question of, "What do you want to be when you grow up?" to now asking "Where are you going to college?"

For every young person in America, whatever their background, one of the essential purposes of schooling should be to help them develop the knowledge and skills needed to search for and obtain work that they find satisfying.[18] But instead, when students finally make it into a college classroom, most arrive without any career direction or idea of what they want to get out of their collegiate education.

But research shows that students who enter college with an informed declared major are far more likely to take the right classes and graduate - by double - than those who wander through the maze of educational choices.[19]

We need a paradigm shift of *choosing a career before choosing a college*. We should no longer ask high school students, "What college do you want to attend?", or "What will be your major?" Instead, we should help a young person by asking them "What career do you want to enter into?" followed by "What skills do you need to acquire?" Only after students choose a broad career focus by working through a comprehensive and meaningful guidance process will they be able to select the right post-secondary option for them.

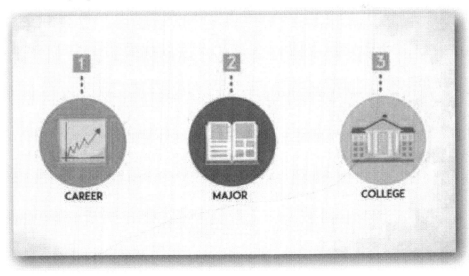

This simple flip of the college decision-making paradigm is the first step in how every student in America should approach their education. Students are more likely to complete their post-secondary education or training if they enter college with three things:

- First: A carefully considered career path
- Second: An informed major or affordable training program that match their career and life goals[20]
- And third: a unique Skills-based Education Plan that facilitates successful entry into the job market

Diane Hollems from "Get Focused, Stay Focused" published an article with the Huffington Post under the title, "Flipping the College Decision-Making Paradigm." We later turned it into an animated video (check it out!). She and her team helped me see the simplistic genius of flipping the college decision-making paradigm as the first step to ensuring all students are prepared for a self-sustaining future.

14. Utilize Skills-Based Education Plans

There's an unspoken belief that the job market is just waiting for hordes of ambitious, eager young graduates to slide into high-paying jobs in the corner office. But, the statistics tell a different story. How is it possible that both college graduates and unfilled job openings are both at record-breaking highs? That seems very counter intuitive. But recently, one in four employers have experienced losses in revenue as a result of not being able to fill open positions. They simply can't find applicants with the necessary skills required in today's workplace. This is known as the skills gap.

To fix this problem, our high schools and colleges must shift their focus from simply degree acquisition by taking a prescribed series of courses to promoting skills acquisition through varied learning opportunities. And not just any skills, but the skills that match those required for the chosen career path of the individual.

A Skills-Based Education Plan illustrates that not all skills can be obtained inside a classroom; and it develops the habit of continuously identifying new skills in order to remain employable. In most fields, students will continue to seek formal degrees; but we also now have access to a growing range of flexible learning alternatives: such as online courses, reading books by top experts, and video tutorials.

Here's one example: If a student's career plan includes holding a political office, they might eventually want to run for mayor of their local city. The traditional path could be to focus on specific courses to earn a college degree in Political Science with a possible minor in Communication. But does a high GPA alone mean they would be qualified to be the mayor? Of course not. The degree itself is important, but insufficient. Rather than approaching the question in the context of a traditional education plan, start by thinking about the skills one would need to become a successful elected official.

One might need to learn public speaking and how to talk on camera through a Toastmasters program, and understand government budgeting by interning for a city council member. Gaining experience in social branding would be helpful, and that could be achieved through a marketing class at the community college. Managing volunteers door-to-door collecting voter registrations would also be valuable experience. It would also be important to learn how to write solicitation letters and understand how to persuade others into action; so in addition to a traditional writing course they might plan to volunteer for a charitable organization's fund raising campaign.

Certainly the most successful politicians are not always the most academically knowledgeable. The most successful are those who have figured out how to hone multiple skills obtained in a variety of ways. We can take that same approach and apply it to all careers.

There are many benefits to adopting Skills-based Education Plans within our institutions:

- Counselors can become architects of human development rather than simply schedulers of classes.

- When liberal arts instructors connect the transferrable skills taught to the real world, their courses become more relevant and therefore motivating.

- And students will graduate with the skills necessary to compete in today's job market improving both the college's reputation and enrollments.

A Skills-Based Education plan is necessary for anyone who wants to avoid the pitfalls of unemployment, or underemployment, after graduation. It puts a students' future in focus towards gaining the skills, aptitudes and attitudes necessary to be competitive in today's job market.

15. Develop more Partnership Academies and Career Pathways

The research is clear that career pathways and partnership academies keep students engaged in school, help contextualize educational content, and prepare students for the world of word. There are many terms, structures, and approaches, but the spirit of this approach is to provide students with a structured sequence of classes that relate to the same occupational/industry focus.

For example, California's state-funded Career Academies, the California Partnership Academies (CPAs), are defined by CA Education Code sections 54690-54699. These three or four-year programs based in public comprehensive high schools are intended in part to meet the needs of at-risk students, and require at least 50% at-risk enrollment. Each CPA has a specific industry focus, with a team of academic and career-technical teachers that share a common planning period, integrate instruction across disciplines, and coordinate support systems. Students enter voluntarily and are scheduled as a cohort in three core academic and one career-technical course in grades 10 and 11 (and sometimes grade 9), and at least one core academic and career-technical course in grade 12.[12] The term Career Pathway is sometimes used synonymously with the term Career Academy. Both include a course sequence of career technical courses. A Career Pathway is a coherent sequence of rigorous academic and technical courses that allows students to apply academics and develop technical skills in a career field. Career pathways prepare students for completion of state academic and technical standards and more advanced postsecondary course work related to the selected career.[22]

Similarly, Career Academies are a school-within-a-school or program combining academic and career technical education courses framed around a career theme intended to prepare high school students for both college and careers. Career Academies, which operate in many states and cities, usually in grades 9-12 or 10-12, use cohort scheduling, create a family-like atmosphere, have partnerships with employers and the community to provide work-based learning, and have relationships with nearby colleges to provide dual-enrollment courses and post-secondary articulation. Academy teachers usually have common planning time to develop interdisciplinary projects and resolve issues with their shared students. Rigorous evaluations have shown academies to have positive impacts on both school performance and employment.[23]

Whatever nomenclature or structure your state adopts, every high school in America should have 2-5 partnership academies, or career pathways, for students to choose from.

16. Delete the Mean

One of my pet peeves is seeing occupational posters, websites, or flyers that list occupations with an average wage next to each job title. The intent to show students the average wage for each occupation is good, but damaging. When displaying just an average, median, or mean wage, students are not getting the full picture. Printing the mean salary implies that everyone earns that same amount. But most students are not the average. They each have skills and deficiencies; they are talented in some areas and struggle in others. They themselves will most likely not earn the average salary. Students often forget that 50% of workers earn more than the published salary, and 50% earn less.

We all know there is great variability of earnings within every job categories. For example, not all teachers earn the same amount of money.

A number of variables affect a teacher's salary including where it is located, the school district, whether it is a public or private school, if the teacher has a certain credential or not, level of education completed, grade level, etc. Instead of simply listing that the average K-12 teacher in America earns $56,383, publish that the range of earnings for K-12 teachers is $39,580 – 75,279.[24] Publishing the wage range will naturally lead one to ask what it takes to earn near the top of that scale instead of near the bottom. Peaking one's curiosity in this way can lead to an earnest career exploration process across all industries.

I recommend publishing wage ranges from the 10th to the 90th percentile to show students the broadest possible spectrum of what exists in the labor market. If that is not available to you, a viable alternative is to publish the 25th to the 75th percentile which represents the middle 50% of workers in a given occupation. Also, definitely add an asterisk after the wage range that explains the data displayed.

If you want to really take it to the next level, also help students think about what they will enjoy and what they will actually be good at doing. Include the skills and personalities which top earners possess. Some community colleges publish their majors along with the Holland Codes which most closely align with the dominant personalities in each field. This is a superb strategy for assisting the undeclared student to think about which majors, and which occupations, may align well with his/her strengths.

17. Don't Follow Your Passion, But Always Bring it With You

I've been in contact with Thomas Frank of College Info Geek where he has talked at length about how "follow your passion" is really the worst advice we can give students today. [25]

Think about it; how many of you have heard someone say that you should "do what you love," and "follow your passion?" Perhaps you often give that advice yourself. In today's society, we are telling our students to find what they love and then plan to do that for a living. Forget about that "unfulfilling" work your grandparents did – instead, follow your passion!

Actually, following your passion is bad advice. First of all, it assumes that everyone has a pre-existing passion. For a small few, this is true. Some people just know from an early age that music is their thing or creating art or even engineering. So for those students, this is excellent advice! But most people have no idea what their passion is – even people who are nearing retirement age. Others have several passions and are interested in a wide variety of things but couldn't begin to tell you which one was THE passion.

Students have little life experience. If an adult has trouble defining their passion, can you imagine the trouble a student will have? What terrible advice to tell them that passion is the answer when most people never can define that for themselves. It makes them feel they have missed out on something prior, are behind their peers, and often makes them feel bad about who they are.

Instead of following their passion, we should suggest to students something Cal Newport said in his book *So Good They Can't Ignore You*, which is to "pick something you have an interest in and simply work as hard as you can to get good at it."[26] The truth is that focusing on skills and gaining experience is the best way to discover what one's passion may be...and subsequently what kind of occupation will make your students feel fulfilled.

To further illustrate this point, Mark Cuban, billionaire entrepreneur and one of the sharks on the TV show *Shark Tank*, wrote a blog post in March 2012 entitled "Don't Follow your Passion, Follow your Effort."[27] He wrote: "When you work hard at something you become good at it. When you become good at doing something, you will enjoy it more. When you enjoy doing something, there is a very good chance you will become passionate or more passionate about it." You see hard work comes first, then enjoyment, followed by passion. Few of us start with passion. Passion is actually a byproduct of focused time, dedication and hard work. Mark concluded his blog by stating, "When you are good at something, passionate, and work even harder to excel and be the best at it, good things happen. Don't follow your passions, follow your effort. It will lead you to your passions and to success, however you define it." Well said Mark.

No one is born to do just one thing. Instead, we are born with personality traits that move us towards certain kinds of work. Your student will discover these qualities as they learn new skills, meet new people, have new experiences, and create new things. In order to discover who they are and what they want to be, they are going to have to do something rather than just think about something.

There's another reason that passion isn't the right advice to follow. It is called boredom. Most things are fun and exciting when you first try them, but eventually, they get boring. If your student only considers the fun behind an activity and what they like to do, then when it gets boring or difficult they are likely to quit and find something new, repeating this process over and over and over again.

Your student will have to learn to push through this boredom and difficulty while they are developing new skills. But, once they have the skills they will find that they are better than many of their peers. Their experience will qualify them for better jobs and more responsibilities. They will find that they are given more interesting assignments because they have learned how to handle them. At this point, the job becomes even more fun.

Passions are difficult to define. Passions can be plentiful, they can wane, or they can not result in a meaningful career. Passion rarely, if ever, comes first. But skills developed through hard work can result in passion and help in securing a career that is fulfilling.

As Mike Rowe once wrote on his Facebook page, "Passion is too important to be without, but too fickle to be guided by. Which is why I'm more inclined to say, Don't Follow Your Passion, But Always Bring it With You."[28]

———

So, as you can see, there are many things educators can do to change the way education is happening in our schools today. Some actions are as simple as attending a meeting. Others are more difficult but provide the opportunity to educate those making policies about the reality of the world of work. If every parent and educator diligently worked towards any two of these 17 suggestions, we would see student-centered policies and paradigms changing to reflect the 21st century economy.

1 California Department of Education Fact Sheet for School Leaders. http://www.cde.ca.gov/ci/ct/gi/cteschoolleaderfacts.asp

2 Plank et al., Dropping Out of High School and the Place of Career and Technical Education, National Research Center for CTE, 2005

3 Office of Career, Technical and Adult Education data; Civic Enterprises et al., Building a Grad Nation: Progress and Challenge in Ending the High School Dropout Epidemic: Annual Update, 2014)

4 https://www.acteonline.org/cte/#.VmnrDLiDGko. CTE Works for High School Students.

5 Lekes et al., CTE Pathway Programs, Academic Performance and the Transition to College and Career, National Research Center for CTE, 2007; SHRM and WSJ.com/Careers, Critical Skills Needs and Resources for the Changing Workforce, 2008

6 http://www.apprenticeshipcarolina.com/resources.html

7 http://www.apprenticeshipcarolina.com/downloads/Apprenticeship-Tax-Credit-Form.pdf

8 http://www.apprenticeshipcarolina.com/resources.html

9 http://www.apprenticeshipcarolina.com/by-the-numbers.html

10 http://education.ohio.gov/Topics/Career-Tech/Career-Connections

11 http://education.ohio.gov/getattachment/Topics/Career-Tech/Career-Connections/Career-Connections-Brochure_Educator_061115.pdf.aspx

12 Watters, Audrey (September 8, 2011). "Master a new skill? Here's your badge". O'Reilly Radar. Retrieved November 21, 2012.

13 http://www.usnews.com/news/blogs/data-mine/2014/10/07/college-board-ap-exam-pass-rate-nearly-doubles-in-10-years#

14 http://www.cde.ca.gov/ta/ac/ar/aprfaq15.asp

15 http://www.forbes.com/sites/uhenergy/2015/12/22/certificates-credentials-and-college-degrees-time-to-shift-our-thinking/2/#2715e4857a0b6ea168f56d43

16 http://money.cnn.com/2015/10/19/technology/schools-innovation/#

17 U.S. Census Bureau, Decennial Census and American Community Survey, U.S. Department of Labor, O*NET. Calculated by the Federal Reserve Bank of New York. 2014. https://www.newyorkfed.org/medialibrary/media/research/current_issues/ci20-1.pdf

18 Hoffman, Nancy. (Nov 2015). High school in Switzerland blends work with learning. The Phi Delta Kappan, *vol. 97 no. 3 29-33.* Phi Delta Kappa International. http://pdk.sagepub.com/content/97/3/29.full?ijkey=mbwHvmbtrQ7sg&keytype=ref&siteid=sppdk.

19 CCCCO Student Success Task Force: http://www.californiacommunitycolleges.cccco.edu/portals/0/executive/studentsuccesstaskforce/sstf_final_report_1-17-12_print.pdf

20 Symonds W.C., Schwartz R., Ferguson R.F.(2011). *Pathways to prosperity: Meeting the challenge of preparing young Americans for the 21st century.* Cambridge, MA: Harvard University Graduate School of Education, Pathways to Prosperity Project

21 www.cde.ca.gov/ci/gs/hs/cpagen.asp

22 www.cord.org/ career-pathways/

23 http://ccasn.berkeley.edu

24 National Center for Eduction Statistics. Tables and Figures. 2013 Table 211.60. Estimated average annual salary of teachers in public elementary and secondary schools, by state. https://nces.ed.gov/programs/digest/d13/tables/dt13_211.60.asp

25 http://collegeinfogeek.com/stop-trying-to-find-your-passion/
26 So Good They Can't Ignore You: Why Skills Trump Passion in the Quest for Work You Love. Cal Newport. 2012
27 http://genius.com/Mark-cuban-dont-follow-your-passion-follow-your-effort-annotated
28 Mike Rowe. Oct 6, 2014. http://freebeacon.com/culture/mike-rowe-on-following-your-passion/

CHAPTER 9

STARTING IN THE RIGHT PLACE AND ASKING THE RIGHT QUESTIONS

Tyranny Vs Genius

There is a highly regarded business author by the name of Jim Collins who wrote both *Good to Great* and *Built to Last*. He was on the New York Times best-seller lists for business for years. A quote of his that I particularly love is, "Successful organizations understand the genius of the 'and' versus the tyranny of the 'or.'"[1] Collins defines the *tyranny of the OR* as the rational view that cannot easily accept paradox; that cannot live with two seemingly contradictory forces or ideas at the same time. *The tyranny of the OR* makes people believe that things must be either A or B, but not both.

Our education system has embraced the "or" for years. You're either going to be a college-bound student OR a career and technical education (CTE) student. You can take a foreign language OR an engineering class. You can take college-prep courses OR earn an industry credential. The way our education system is measured forces a false dichotomy, suggesting that students need to be either CTE OR college bound.

Moreover, in many systems, two different types of counselors are being employed: general academic counselors and career counselors. Talk about the tyranny of the "or." In such systems, students are told if you want help with your academic planning, go to the academic counselor. If you want help with CTE or finding a job, go to the career counselor.

This false dichotomy makes no sense because such sharp lines of distinction no longer exist. They have become blurred both in our educational system and in the real world. In the 21st century, many CTE programs do provide college preparation and/or result in transferable credit, just as many university-bound programs contain technical skills. Fortunately, there is a better paradigm. To truly fix our educational system, we must instead adopt what Jim Collins calls the *Genius of the AND*. This is the ability to embrace and allow both extremes.

The Genius of the AND is to say to students, "Yes, you may earn your industry certification AND take college-preparation classes." "You must enroll in a CTE class AND a foreign language to graduate." "To earn a good job, you will need both a strong foundation in reading, writing, and math AND will need technical skills which are in-demand in today's labor market." All students deserve to be career minded AND college minded.

And Then Some

In public education, counselors are expected to do certain things. They have to meet all the standards. They have to help those on academic probation and get them through. My good friend Dr. Charles Lee-Johnson worked as both a high school counselor and a community college counselor. He often states that counselors are asked to monitor the parking lot, graduation rates, and discipline files simultaneously. Counselors have to deal with a number of measures and processes. Of course, all of this is useful and needful. However, to be great counselors, one needs to be "and then some."

Look at it this way. If you want to make a copy of a piece of paper, instead of saying, "I want to copy the paper, you say I want to Xerox it." Xerox is the name of a brand, but you say Xerox because they did copies so well that they became synonymous with copying. The same thing happened with tissues. If you want to blow your nose, you ask for Kleenex. Kleenex is a brand that became synonymous with tissues. Both companies have the "and then some" quality. They defined an entire industry by their brand and their reputation.

What I'm suggesting is that all of us need to be educators - and then some. Instead of doing the bare minimum and guiding students to classes that fit the one size fits all paradigm, let's redefine the role and in so doing let's redefine public education in America. Let's redefine counselors and educators as those who help students find a career path that fits their individual needs and aptitudes. Let's embrace the Genius of the AND.

The Wrong Question

As mentioned previously, career planning usually just consists of the question, "What do you want to be when you grow up?" Nothing much else is said on the subject and students are left to fend for themselves as they try to figure out the answer to the question.

In addition to leaving them on their own for career exploration, we are giving them the wrong kind of information even with the one question we ask. Asking them what they want to be when they grow up suggests that there is one right answer and that they need to discover this answer at a young age! It is simply no longer the right question. Studies show that students graduating today will have between 15 and 20 jobs over the course of their life.[2] Some studies suggest as many as 40 jobs!

Sometimes these changes are just job changes, such as being a salesman for one company and then moving to being a salesman in a different company. Other times, it is a total career change, such as going from a teacher to a business consultant, or a lawyer to a journalist.

Why are people changing jobs more now than in the past? Here are just a few reasons:[3]

- Looking for higher pay
- More likely to relocate to another location
- Looking for career advancement
- Looking for less stress
- Company reorganization
- Layoffs
- Looking for something more interesting
- Wanting more recognition
- Outsourcing

The Bureau of Labor and Statistics says it is difficult to determine when someone has changed careers or just changed jobs.[4] For instance, if a teacher becomes a sales trainer, is she still a teacher or did she change careers? You could argue this both ways. She is still teaching in both instances but no longer working with children. On the other hand, she is now working in a business sector, so that is a change of careers. This means that the data on career changes is fuzzy at best.

But what we do know is this: The idea of getting in on the ground floor of a company, staying there 40 years, and retiring with a gold watch is no longer the way our economy works. Instead, people start with one job, move to another occupation that most likely involves some transferable but different skills, which then later evolves into some different position with expended skills and knowledge. Eventually, 20 years and 10 jobs later, what they started out doing no longer looks like what they do today.

Career Planning the Right Way

This means that we don't need to ask our students what they want to be when they grow up. Instead, the question should be, "What do you think you'd like to do first?"

As your students grow and learn and have experiences, they will begin to combine various interests that lead them to shift around in their employment, always looking to find the right fit. The truth is the factors that make a career satisfying change over time and with circumstances. A satisfying job at the age of 32 may no longer be satisfying at 47.

Additionally, jobs and the nature of jobs changes over time. Who would have thought in 1995 that social media marketing specialists would be a thing? New jobs and even entire job categories are constantly being created. In 2014, SocialStrategi.com reviewed 259 million LinkedIn profiles to find jobs that hadn't been around just five years before. Those on the list included:[5]

- IOS Developer – In 2008, there were fewer than 100 IOS developers on LinkedIn. In 2013, there were over 12,000.

- Android Developer – Like the IOS developer, this increased from less than 100 jobs to more than 10,000 in five years.
- Zumba Instructor – In 2008, Zumba did not exist on LinkedIn. This position grew 396 times in 5 years.
- Social Media Intern – Increased 174 times in five years
- Data Scientist – Just 142 people on LinkedIn were making sense of digital information in 2008. Today, there are over 4,000 people listed as data scientists.
- UI/UX Designer – Demand increased 22 times
- Big Data Architect – this occupation barely existed. It has grown an astonishing 3,440 times in 5 years!
- Beachbody Coach – Coaching and distributing fitness products by Beachbody has increased over 3,000 times.
- Cloud Services Specialist – Growth of 17 times in 5 years
- Digital Marketing Specialist – Also a growth of 17 times in 5 years

But what of the future? FutureTimeline.net suggests the following emerging job titles for 2030:[6]

- Alternative Vehicle Developer
- Avatar Manager
- Body Part Maker
- Climate Change Reversal Specialist
- Memory Augmentation Surgeon
- Nano Medic
- Narrowcaster
- 'New Science' Ethicist
- Old Age Wellness Manager
- Quarantine Enforcer
- Social Networking Officer
- Space Pilot
- Vertical Farmer
- Virtual Clutter Organizer
- Virtual Lawyer
- Virtual Teacher
- Waste Data Handler

This future look is why it is so necessary to start with a plan for an initial career. This will not only help a student know where to land when they are finished with post-secondary education, but it will also help them know what to do if they determine that a job shift later in life is what is needed. They will realize that they don't need to have the answer to the question, "What will make me happy in 40 years?" That question produces too much anxiety. Instead, they can focus on the near future, get into the workforce, and continue to grow and evolve as circumstances, needs, and desires dictate.

To help with this idea of career exploration and planning, many schools have started what is known as the Get Focused...Stay Focused! (GFSF) Initiative.[7] Students at more than 150 schools throughout the nation are flipping the college decision-making paradigm. In this program, freshmen complete a semester or two of classes that help them identify their interests and goals and then find careers that align to those interests and goals. Then these students create a 10-year education plan. Each subsequent year, the students take follow-up modules to help them update and revise their plan, expand their options, select post-secondary training, and identify needed skills.

But, not all schools can dedicate an entire class to this vital process. So, I helped create an interactive curriculum entitled Dream Catcher that is comprised of just 8 innovative lessons. Dream Catcher is a workforce and career development curriculum that helps students identify their purpose in life and achieve their career dreams. Designed for 7th grade through adulthood, this flexible curriculum is divided into two modules: Self and Career Exploration and then Life and Career Experience. Each module is independent and can be taught as stand-alone units, and can be easily integrated into any classroom, after school group, or home schooling curriculum. My goal is to make this the most affordable, hopefully someday free, purpose-driven career curriculum in America. (Shameless plug: check us out at www.TelosES.com.)

What do all these types of programs accomplish?[8]

1. Students intentionally explore and learn about themselves and their strengths
2. Students carefully consider multiple possible career paths

3. Students are less likely to drop out of high school because they see the relevance in their school work

4. Students experience increased intrinsic motivation for their schooling

5. Students make an informed decision about a major or program of study

6. Students get post-secondary training/education that matches their career and goals

7. Students are more likely to be hired after post-secondary training/education because the skills they have match what employers are seeking

As you can see, when we start with the right questions, we are more likely to get the right answers. Students will be more satisfied with their schooling, will come out of the process with a "good job" as individually defined by them, will not have debt for classes that were worthless to their career choice, and will be happier overall.

As parents and educators, we need to help our students focus on the right goals and create a plan that will lead them to success. Each plan will be unique because each student is unique. The one way to win will no longer be a 4-year university education in anything. Instead, the best way to win will be to an individualized plan tailored to personality, skills, interests, and the labor market.

The Right Questions

It's no longer just enough to encourage our high school students to graduate from high school. It's also no longer just enough to discuss with them about getting into post-secondary education. We need to push the goal post even further down the field; not just to get into post-secondary education, but to complete it. But even this is not enough. The real goal should be ensuring our students have a successful career and a successful life regardless of their path immediately after high school. If that's the end goal, and if that's the touchdown, then we need to change the name of the game. We also need to change the questions we ask.

We've been focused on access to college for so long that we are no longer doing the job that students need us to do. We aren't serving our students as well as we could be. You can have the best, most detailed map of Topeka, Kansas, but if you're trying to navigate through Orlando, Florida, your map is absolutely useless. We're spending a lot of time creating beautiful, accurate academic maps for students, but these maps aren't being followed and aren't relevant to where most students are heading.

CTE is to some teens what AP and honors courses are to others. One is no longer an alternative to the other. They really are different, but equal, pathways...often guiding different students to the same place via very divergent paths. To get students, parents, and policy makers to understand these equal paths, it is time we ask the right questions.

Recently I was talking with an advisor in the North Carolina Community College system who works with kids planning to go to UNC-Chapel Hill through a program called C-Step. When he starts working with these students, many come in with the idea of being a doctor, nurse, lawyer, business manager, or teacher. Why? Well, these are jobs that are known quantities. The students have some notion as to what this job entails and feel they can get a job when they graduate.

He was really astonished by the number of girls, in particular, that came into the program wanting to be a nurse. When he started asking them questions, they really hadn't considered much beyond the idea that nurses were in demand and they would be able to have a job. They had not considered whether they were "right" for the job. They had not considered the dozens of other career options within the healthcare sector. Many had not even considered what it would be like to take care of sick people.

This is not atypical. A high school counselor talked with me about a girl that came into his office wanting to go to a particular college based on the fact that they had "fashion" classes. He asked her if her interest was in fashion design or merchandising and she had no idea that there was a difference. After some career exploration, she realized that the college she had chosen was not her best choice since it didn't reflect what she wanted to do.

None of these students had been asked or been asking themselves the right questions. But as you have learned, when you start with the right questions, you are bound to get to the right answers.

1 Jim Collins. Building Companies to Last. 1995. http://www.jimcollins.com/article_topics/articles/building-companies.html

2 http://futureworkplace.com/wp-content/uploads/MultipleGenAtWork_infographic.pdf

3 Global Job Seeker Trends: Why & How People Change Jobs. LinkedIn Talent Solutions. 2015

4 Bureau of Labor and Statistics. http://www.bls.gov/nls/nlsfaqs.htm#anch43

5 http://www.socialstrategi.com/10-most-popular-new-job-titles/

6 http://www.futuretimeline.net/21stcentury/2030.htm#career

7 http://getfocusedstayfocused.org/

8 http://gettingsmart.com/2015/11/flipping-the-college-decision-making-paradigm/

CHAPTER 10

SIX STEPS TO STUDENT SUCCESS

Step One: Self-Exploration

I suggest a six-step program to help students determine their educational and eventual career path. First, we must help the students start with self-exploration.

Part of this step includes first understanding who your students are from multiple lenses. For example, my friend Charles' wife is from Belize. In Belizean culture, women are not supposed to go to school. They are supposed to find a man, get married, have kids and take care of the house. In fact, girls who are not married by 19 are looked at oddly, and the family begins to worry. As educators, we don't like to talk about these things, but they are real.

Our students come to us with cultural challenges. As we try to guide them, they are also getting advice from home. Perhaps your student wants to go into welding and get his Associate in Applied Science in Industrial Automation. He is all excited, but when he tells his parents, they tell him, "That's not a real major. You'll never make any money doing that. I didn't work as hard as I have for you to go to school for that major. You are going to college to become a doctor!" So, your student hangs his head, comes back to you and says that he has to be a doctor despite the fact that being a doctor isn't what he had in mind. We need to acknowledge and understand that often times college and career decisions are made collectively as opposed to individually. Thus, educating parents simultaneously is so vital to this process.

Cultural differences are another reason why the first step must be one of self-exploration, as well as a helping the student build self-esteem. Getting someone to understand who they are and feel good about that is the number one factor for performance. The better they feel about themselves, the better they will do in life.[1]

It is important for your students to recognize key characteristics about themselves so they can make informed career choices that are well suited for them. It is amazing to me how many hours someone will put into researching new cars before buying, yet spend very little time researching a career. Educational choices based on career choices are much costlier than a new car and the effects of a poor choice can stick around for a lot longer.

The first question to ask students is, "What do you like to do?" To answer this question, your student can identify their hobbies, as well as things they enjoy talking about or learning about. Anything that naturally captures their attention should go on this list. For most students, this will be varied and could include things like photography, science fiction movies, video games, and Civil War history.

Once they have answers to that, the next question is, "What are you good at doing?" Note that this is a separate question entirely. A student may want to be starting quarterback in the NFL, but may stand 5 feet tall. Perhaps a student loves music and wants to be a rock star, but quite frankly isn't very good.

The answer to this question will indicate the student's skills and abilities and, in some cases, the student's perception of reality. These are typically things that they do well on naturally but can also include skills and strengths they have acquired through experience and training. Having a clear understanding of their skill sets and how they would prefer to use these skills helps your student to choose career fields that best fit their strengths.

Many like to quote the Confucius saying, "Choose a job you love, and you will never have to work a day in your life." This is very sage advice, but it is incomplete, as we discovered when talking about passions.

Additionally, another piece of bad advice is "You can be anything you want to be." This advice is very well-intentioned but completely misleading. Instead, we should be saying, "You can try anything you want...but not everything." Or taking that slightly further, "you should try and explore anything and everything, but will be most successful doing something you enjoy which is in alignment with your core talents and strengths."

Tom Rath, author of *StrengthFinder 2.0* writes, "You cannot be anything you want to be, but you can be a lot more of who you already are."[2] Anyone that has studied personality traits and psychology theories knows there is a great deal of truth to this.

The strength finder study (StrengthsQuest) focuses on 34 themes and ideas for actions in categories where people fall under categories such as activator, intellect, and harmony. It is rooted in positive psychology and has a strong research background utilizing a strength-based model, as opposed to a deficit based approach. Now, I don't necessarily believe this is the silver bullet assessment for self-awareness, but I think having students take this in addition to others can be a very valuable tool for understanding how strengths and personalities can be used most effectively in academic and career planning.

Another part of self-exploration is to determine how they want their ideal life to look. You will want to discuss areas of interest and aptitudes. You will want to know how they define success. And finally, you will want to discuss the lifestyle they want to lead. Ask questions such as, "Where would you like to live?", "Do you like city life or country life?", "Do you want a family?", and "Are there things that are important to where you live such as the location of religious worship, hobbies such as skiing, or medical facilities?" If a student has a preference to live in a certain area, understanding the needs for that area will be important when considering occupations.

Have them describe what they'd like to do, where they'd like to live, how they'd like to spend their time and with whom, and what skills, training, and interests they wish to develop. This is not yet the time to talk about specific careers. Instead, first focus on life and what a good life looks like.

A great example of a website that helps to facilitate this exploration in a fun and interactive way is the California CareerZone (www.CaCareerZone.org). Websites like this help students to see the connection between what they say they want in life with the job they choose. For example, if they say they want to live in Malibu but are thinking about being the director of a local nonprofit organization, they may need assistance seeing see that their lifestyle goals and career plans are not well aligned.

Here are two good resources for self-exploration that I have used and vetted. Additional resources are listed in Appendix E, most of which are free:

> O'Net Online Skills Search: This allows students to choose skills from six different skill groups including basic skills, complex problem-solving skills, resource management skills, social skills, systems skills, and technical skills. https://www.onetonline.org/skills/
>
> Career InfoNet Skills Profiler: This allows students to choose from seven different skill groups including basic skills, social skills, complex problem-solving skills, technical skills, system skills, resource management skills, and desktop computer skills. http://www.careerinfonet.org/skills/skills_list.aspx

Step Two: Personality Assessment

Once self-exploration is completed, the second step is personality assessment to be sure that the personality of the student will align with future career choices. Studies have shown that people find a career the most satisfying when it fits with their own style of operation. Learning about their personality traits, personal qualities, and work environment preferences will help your students understand what motivates them and brings them the most satisfaction. This will help them make career and educational choices that suit who they are.

There are hundreds of personality tests available. The Holland Code and Myers-Briggs Type Indicator (MBTI) are among the most popular. Many career centers offer these (or similar) assessments to help a student understand the way they perceive the world and interact with others. Ask the question, "What careers are typically a good fit for those with my personality preferences?" Choose a few of the best tests to help them identify where they can thrive given the type of person they are.

Some personality tests to consider are:

CA CareerZone Interest Profiler: Occupational interests are identified through a series of questions about work activities that some people do on their jobs. Based on the aforementioned Holland Code, it includes comprehensive information on over 900 occupations. https://www.cacareerzone.org/ip/
Jung Typology Test: Helps identify one's lifestyle preferences, personality strengths, and suitably aligned career choices.
http://www.humanmetrics.com/
Myers-Briggs Type Indicator (MBTI): This personality test builds upon Jung's typologies and is one of the most reliable and trusted. It has been selected by the nation's top colleges to help with career development and is backed by scientific research.[3] This test will help your students understand themselves and how they interact with others. It will help them identify their preferences in four areas: where they focus their attention, how they take in information, how they make decisions based on the information, and how they deal with the world. The original test costs $49.95, however, a free version can be found at http://www.truity.com/test/type-finder-research-edition.

Step Three: Career Exploration

Now that they understand their skills and personality, it is time to look at what careers are available that match. The right questions to ask for step three are, "What can you get paid to do?", "Can we combine interest and ability with an occupational opportunity to get paid?" and "What occupations and industries are high-priority and/or emerging?" At this point, the student begins to look at actual job activities available to them which also align with their interests and strengths.

It is vital for students to see the connection between careers and personality. I recently met a college student who was studying accounting and was almost ready to graduate with her Associates Degree. As we talked, she revealed that she wasn't really good with numbers, had below-average grades, and was nervous about interacting with people all the time. Hearing that, I asked why it was she wanted to be an accountant. As expected she replied, "because CPAs make a lot of money." With all the grace I could muster I gave a small smile and softly replied, "Sorry my friend, but you probably wont." After thirty minutes of conversation and soul searching, she understood the necessity of aligning who she was with her chosen profession. She realized not everyone in a given occupation earns the same amount of money regardless of skill, and that personality fit was a pivotal ingredient for ensuring success in a fulfilling career.

My wife's grandmother tells a quintessential story of career exploration that changed the trajectory of her life. As newlyweds, she and her husband applied to be missionaries in Oraibi, Arizona and were accepted. They were thrilled at the prospect of getting a young Christian couple to run their education system since he was a school administrator and she was an elementary school teacher. Quite the catch! All they needed was a recommendation from their pastor. To their surprise, he withheld it. He would not give them the requested recommendation. His reason was that while her husband could adjust to that lifestyle, she was "never meant to live on the back side of the desert." In retrospect, she was deeply appreciative of his wisdom and caring by refusing to comply with their uninformed desires. He was right; and it changed their lives.

From a financial perspective, refer back to the student's envisioned future lifestyle. Ask them, "What type of realistic income would you like to earn?" and "How much would you need to sustain your envisioned lifestyle?" and "What careers would enable you to earn that type of income?" The goal is to begin to align their desired lifestyle, with their personality, and with careers that could financially support their vision.

But where to start? The Department of Labor says there are nearly 1,000 different jobs available.[4] That's a lot of occupations to explore. If your students chose one per day, it would take three years to explore them all! Instead of exploring every job, have your students start with job clusters. Clusters contain occupations in the same field of work that require similar skills across every educational level of obtainment. Organizing career exploration by career clusters makes the task more enjoyable and more manageable.

The Occupational Outlook Handbook suggests these 25 categories:

1. Architecture and Engineering
2. Arts and Design
3. Building and Grounds Cleaning,
4. Business and Financial
5. Community and Social Service
6. Computer and Information Technology
7. Construction and Extraction
8. Education, Training, and Library
9. Entertainment and Sports
10. Farming, Fishing, and Forestry
11. Food Preparation and Serving
12. Healthcare
13. Installation, Maintenance, and Repair
14. Legal
15. Life, Physical, and Social Science
16. Management
17. Math
18. Media and Communication
19. Military
20. Office and Administrative Support
21. Personal Care and Service
22. Production
23. Protective Service
24. Sales
25. Transportation and Material Moving

Another widely used cluster schematic endorsed by the United States Department of Education uses the following 16 industry clusters:

1. Agriculture, Food, and Natural Resources
2. Architecture and Construction
3. Arts, Audio/Video Technology, and Communications
4. Business, Management, and Administration
5. Education and Training

6. Finance
7. Government and Public Administration
8. Health Science
9. Hospitality and Tourism
10. Human Services
11. Information Technology
12. Law, Public Safety, Corrections, and Security
13. Manufacturing
14. Marketing, Sales, and Service
15. Science, Technology, Engineering, and Mathematics
16. Transportation, Distribution, and Logistics

Most states also have adapted these clusters (sometimes called industry sectors) to mirror their regional economy and growth sectors. For example, the California CTE system has organized its courses into 15 industry sectors while Hawaii has focused upon six sectors. As an educator, you don't have to be an expert in healthcare, information communication technologies, or in global training logistics, but you can have at your fingertips organized information your student needs to help them make more informed choices.

In addition to the career clusters schema, a free, yet underutilized, strategy for successfully exploring careers is the informational interview. Imagine that you received a phone call out of the blue from a local high school student who said they were interested in learning about your career path, what you liked and didn't like about your job, and how you got to where you are. Imagine they told you they were interested in your field and wanted to be like you when they grew up. If they offered to buy you a soda to learn from you and ask for your advice, wouldn't you say yes? I bet 99% of people would. This is true because most people's favorite topic to discuss is themselves. But most people also want to give back to others and feel flattered when today's youth ask about our personal journey.

Encourage the students in your life to conduct five of these informational interviews to professionals in their field of interest. I guarantee they will learn a lot, and potentially even secure a mentor in the field. If there are no professionals nearby in their field of interest, tell them about the PBS phenomenon Road Trip Nation. If you're not familiar with it, it is worth exploring their expansive online informational interview videos from both current and past seasons.

There are also some good free tests that can help guide a student towards careers given their interests and skills. More are listed in Appendix E, but my favorites are:

Career Interest Profiler: 180-question assessment measures occupation and career interests. http://quintcareers.testingroom.com/

ASVAB - Multiple-choice test that helps a student identify which Army jobs are best for them. The entire test is done through a military recruiting office, but sample tests can be found online. https://www.4tests.com/asvab

In addition to the tests listed above, here are a few free resources that will help you guide your students through the entire career exploration maze:

California Career Café: Created for community college students, this site is free and useful to high school students as well. It helps them identify their strengths, talents, interests and educational options. It also helps students explore careers, connect them to employers, and teach them what soft skills are needed by these employers. http://www.cacareercafe.com/

Dirty Jobs: A Discovery Channel series with Mike Rowe. He assumes the duties of the job he profiles for the week, helping students gain an appreciation for the many different jobs available and what makes people happy in those jobs other consider "too dirty." http://www.discovery.com/tv-shows/dirty-jobs/

O'Net Online: At O'Net, a student can enter a work or title, look up careers by expected job growth, by career cluster, by green economy sector, by industry, by job family, by STEM discipline, and by education, experience, and training necessary. As jobs are located, O'Net provides information about the tasks, tools, technology, knowledge, skills, abilities, work activities, work context, job zone, education, credentials, interests, work styles, work values, related occupations, wages, employment, and job openings. https://www.onetonline.org/

Step Four: Set a Tentative Career Goal

Step four is to set a tentative career goal. This can be very scary for students because they are still stuck on the question, "What do I want to do for the rest of my life?" Most 14-year-olds have no idea. In fact, most 30-year-olds have no idea!

Since this is going to be true for a majority of students, we need to remind our students that they only need to think about what they want to do first; and that this first decision is only tentative. If, after more exploration, they want to make a change, it will be much easier because they already have done steps 1 through 3.

As the saying goes, if you fail to plan then you plan to fail. So, obviously we want to help our students set an initial career goal based off what they learned during steps 1 and 2. But note that a tentative, researched, career goal precedes any education or training decisions.

Step Five: Education/Training Research

Once your student has a tentative/initial career in mind, it is then time to research what it takes to become what they wish to become. For many occupations, there are many paths, so be sure to invite your student to explore all available options which lead to their initial career goal.

This is going to require some out of the box thinking. Most students and their parents automatically assume that a 4-year school is the next step to education. The idea of waiting a year or two before going to college while getting a little job experience may sound crazy to them, as will the idea that they may not need a 4-year college degree at all.

For instance, if a student wants to be an interior designer, they will find that there are certificate programs, 2-year associate programs, and 4-year programs available. When it comes to certifications, there are core, advanced, and specialty courses available. Additionally, the student may want to think about an internship or apprenticeship.

Finally, while in high school, they may want to consider getting a job that uses interior design skills such as merchandise display, wallpaper hanger, or painter. If they can't find work with an interior designer, they could look for work in similar fields such as architecture or floral design. They will also want to consider high school classes that give them the types of skills needed to be an interior designer such as a communications class that will teach them to convey oral information effectively, classes that help them with critical thinking, and classes that teach them geometry skills related to figuring the right amount of paint or wallpaper to order.

Step Six: Establish a Skills-Based Educational Plan

Now that your student has several education pathways that have been researched, they need to choose the one that best suits them. Questions to ask at this final step include, "Will you need formal schooling or specific credentials to get into your career?", "What skills and knowledge do you need to acquire to transition into your initial career?", "What schools offer the programs you will need?", and "Beyond traditional academic programs, what can you do to further your skills and knowledge about the career you've chosen?" They will consider their interest in more schooling, the cost of schooling, the location of training, the amount of money they will make with additional training, the ability to get training while working, along with many other factors.

This plan will be the blueprint for what classes they take in high school, the post-secondary programs they wish to complete, and the institutions they apply to attend. Because of this plan, students will see the reason behind the courses they take and find true relevance to their coursework.

If we work with students in this way, they are much more likely to discover a first career that suits their needs and desires. They are far less likely to pick a college first, pick a major next, and finally try to figure out a career once they've graduated. In fact, these six steps, in the right order, are the secret formula for academic relevancy and initial career success.

This might sound like an odd transition, but I love going to the doctor knowing my file is placed on the outside of the door. When they walk into the room, they already know everything about me. They know my history, current medications, and what's ailing me. Imagine as counselors, if you had all the vitals of your students before they walked in your door. Then when they came in you could say, "Great to meet you. You are a blue, or ISTP. You've done these activities. I know your personality, and I know you lifestyle and career goals. I know where you want to be. I even know the top five industry clusters you want to go into. Now let's talk."

Dream Catcher, my10yearplan.com, and The California Career Center are excellent sources for developing a skills-based education plan that I personally support/endorse. As a free resource, The California Career Center features an easy to develop and modify Career Action Plan. Students can establish a free "My Stuff" student account that includes both a High School Plan and Career Action Plans. The accounts have no expiration date so a student could establish an account in 7 or 8th grade to create a plan for high school, then develop a Career Action Plan to look beyond high school, and return to it as often as they wish during and any time after high school. Plans can be modified as often as students want and easily downloaded as a PDF to be shared with a counselor, teacher, or parent/guardian.

Where it is Currently Succeeding

Career planning is working across the nation in various states and among various school districts. Here are six examples throughout the country to give you a feel for what is happening and what can be possible for your students.

Silverado High School in California has implemented a Freshman transition program sponsored by George Washington University's Freshman Transition Initiative using the Career Choices curriculum. Each ninth grader takes the Freshman Seminar and explores careers they find interesting. They are also encouraged to visualize their life in 10 years, develop a budget based on that lifestyle, and look at careers that can support that lifestyle. Once they know what they want, they research the education and qualifications needed for those careers. This 10-year plan is developed on My10yearPlan.com and is updated twice a year throughout high school. Students in this class increased their GPA by 69%, and 100% of participating students passed the California High School Exit Exam. Additionally, Silverado High School had a decrease is suspensions and dropouts.[5]

In Nebraska this year, schools developed the *Engage* program for middle school aged students.[6] Individual student planning is an important component of the Nebraska system and consists of school counselors coordinating ongoing activities designed to assist students in establishing personal goals and academic and career planning.[7] They believe that the career development process should begin in elementary school and continue throughout a student's life. This intentional learning process includes awareness, exploration, preparation, and application. As part of the program, students will learn what knowledge and skills are necessary for the different career clusters, learn about requirements for post-secondary training, be given learning opportunities that connect information with careers, and develop educational plans.

In Iowa, the Department of Education now requires all students to use a program called "I Have a Plan Iowa."[8] The website www. IHaveaPlanIowa.gov provides free access, information, and resources for all Iowans seeking assistance with career and college planning. In the 8th grade, all students begin a process to determine their interests and help them explore careers based on those interests. Then they create a 5-year academic/career plan that they access and revise throughout their high school years which aligns their coursework with future career interests. Listed below are the state requirements for each grade. Skim the steps for each grade and consider how you could assist students in your sphere of influence to do something similar.

Iowa Required State Components for Career Planning
8th Grade

- Create an electronic student portfolio
- Complete a career interest assessment
- Complete a Career Cluster Assessment and identify a Career Cluster of interest
- Build a course plan for high school/ postsecondary
- A Parent approval and signature form (electronic or printed)

9th Grade

- Complete the Interest Profiler Assessment
- Complete a career assessment linking interests & school subjects
- Complete a skills assessment linking skills and careers
- Revise and rebuild course plan in portfolio
- Complete a student reflection paragraph

10th Grade

- Complete work values/beliefs survey
- Compare careers options side by side
- Research careers and programs
- Compare colleges/programs side by side
- Review and revise course plan in portfolio
- Complete a student reflection paragraph

11th Grade

- Complete a skills inventory, checklist or assessment
- Create a resume
- Create a cover letter
- Compare schools and programs side by side
- Note any postsecondary visits (virtual or physical)
- Complete a practice postsecondary application
- Research financial aid and financial aid information
- Research scholarships and scholarship information
- Review and revise course plan in portfolio
- Complete a student reflection paragraph

12th Grade

- Retake Interest Profiler and compare results with 9th-grade results
- Retake career assessment linking school subjects and careers and compare results with 9th grade
- Review school and colleges and indicate choices
- Research job interview information and complete job interview practice
- Review and revise your career plan and your postsecondary opportunities
- Complete a student reflection paragraph

Ensuring that all students have a high-quality career plan early in their academic studies is paying off for Iowa. Nearly 600,000 unique visitors visited the site over 1,126,000 times to complete electronic portfolios, career assessments, educational and career planning, and gain employability skills.[9] Iowa's four-year graduation rate has climbed statewide for four consecutive years while dropout rates continue to fall. The data show 90.5 percent of high school students in Iowa's class of 2014 graduated within four years.[10] The state's October 2015 Task force Report revalidates the need, and funding, for the successful "I Have a Plan Iowa" program.[11]

California also has an easy to use resource called the Career & College Readiness Lesson Plans. There are 45 lessons beginning in grade 5 and continuing through grade 12. Students will take career assessments, explore career options, develop budgets, learn job search skills, and finish 12th grade with a completed Career Action Plan.[12]

Taking a different approach, the modern version of what an apprenticeship could look like for American students is on display at the Apprentice School in Newport News, Virginia.[13] Students who choose from one of more than twenty occupational areas are paid an annual salary of $54,000 by the final year of the program, which is $10,000 above that of the average bachelor's degree recipient. Plus, afterward they are guaranteed a job with the military contractor that operates Newport News Shipbuilding. The school is just as selective as Harvard. It receives more than 4,000 applications each year for 230 spots, and significant numbers of its graduates go on to earn bachelor's or master's degrees. In many ways, it looks and feels like a typical American college, except in one important respect: its students graduate debt free.

Finally, Oklahoma created a 12-year plan to graduate 20,400 more students from college and CareerTech and they are succeeding beyond their goals.[14] Their Complete College America initiative works to get students to take classes and receive degrees and certificates relevant to Oklahoma's workforce needs. The intent is to attract new jobs and expand the jobs already located in the area. The state network of 29 technology centers is propelling this initiative forward.

———

These six examples help illustrate what we need to evolve towards. We need to walk our students through this process so that every student that walks through our doors can be successful once they graduate. Adding true career planning to the arsenal provided to students as they prepare for their future is the Genius of the AND that all students desperately need.

1   Mohammad Aryana, 2010. Relationship Between Self-esteem and Academic Achievement Amongst Pre-University Students. Journal of Applied Sciences, 10: 2474-2477.
2   StrengthsFinder 2.0. 2007. Tom Rath.
3   https://www.cpp.com/products/mbti/index.aspx
4   "Bureau of Labor Statistics, U.S. Department of Labor, 2014–2015 Occupational Outlook Handbook, [date accessed] [http://www.bls.gov/ooh/]."
5   http://www.academicinnovations.com/dataproof/silveradoslc.pdf
6   http://www.education.ne.gov/cared/Engage.html
7   https://www.acteonline.org/uploadedFiles/Assets_and_Documents/Global/files/Publications/Techniques/2010/tech_oct10_A_Leading_Role_for_Career_and_Guidance_Counselors.pdf
8   https://secure.ihaveaplaniowa.gov/
9   https://www.educateiowa.gov/sites/files/ed/documents/2011-2012%20Student%20Curriculum%20%20%288th%20Grade%29%20Plan%20Annual%20Report.pdf;   and   http://www.dom.state.ia.us/planning_performance/files/reports/FY14/FY14_EducationPerformanceReport.pdf
10 https://www.educateiowa.gov/article/2015/04/01/iowa-s-high-school-graduation-rate-tops-90-percent
11 https://www.educateiowa.gov/sites/files/ed/documents/2015-10-26CTETaskForceFinalReport.pdf
12 CalCRN. https://www.cacareerzone.org
13 Jeff Selingo (March 16, 2016). Author, THERE IS LIFE AFTER COLLEGE, COLLEGE (UN)BOUND. Washington Post Writer, Wanted: A Harvard for Skilled Jobs.
14 http://newsok.com/state-exceeds-college-completion-goal-for-third-year/article/5448577

CONCLUSION

(RE)DEFINING THE GOAL

Remember my friend Mike from Chapter two? Can you imagine his fate if someone in his life had helped him consider career choices sooner? Rather than being an educational success story despite still searching for a career while over $100,000 debt with an unused degree in-hand, he could be a career success story with a job he finds satisfying.

If someone had given him some direction on careers that matched his personality and skill set rather than simply showing him a chart stating that any degree at any college was the next step after graduation, he might have no debt and be pulling in six figures by now. The dialogue and advice he received from both his home and his school were archaic and unchallenged. If he understood his personality and work style first, truly realizing that he was a creative entrepreneur, he may never have strayed into real estate or financial planning. Mike could have focused instead on careers which better aligned with his core talents and strengths.

Success should be defined not by easily calculated numbers like SAT scores or the number of kids enrolling in college, but by numbers that indicate how many students secure gainful employment when they are done with their education/training.

My story ended successfully, but not before I found myself with five degrees, a lot of debt, and finally earning an industry certification. Thirty percent of our high school freshman should not drop out of school because they don't find their courses to be relevant. Fourty-two percent of students should not graduate from high school without getting any further education, especially since we know that most good jobs require some post-secondary training. Of those that do go on to college, 43% should not be dropping out. And of the ones that actually graduate, 46% should not be working in jobs that do not require the degree they have earned.

Rather than send our students out into the world over-educated but unable to function in a career, let's give them a better path that allows more than 7 out of 100 to win. Let's teach them the truth about the skills gap. Let's inform them about the dozens of in-demand jobs available at every education level. Let's also show them how to research the labor market to know what positions will pay upon graduation. Let's show them how to achieve lifelong success by aligning who they are with what the high-paying jobs are in today's economy. Let's redefine success, push the goal post back, and demand that all students have a combination of academic knowledge, career awareness, and technical skills to be successful.

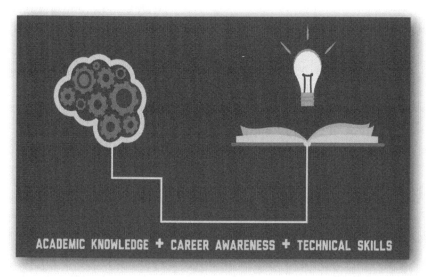

ACADEMIC KNOWLEDGE + CAREER AWARENESS + TECHNICAL SKILLS

We need to stop our addiction to the 4-year university degree for all. It is time to fix the vast disconnect between the way we prepare our students for the world of work and the realities of our economy. There is simply no need for college graduates to be unemployed or underemployed. Similarly, they shouldn't be forced to take positions below the level they were educated for, while buried in a mountain of student loan debt. This won't be an issue if we can teach students how to make an informed career goal before they pick an initial educational path.

If there ever was a time when we could justify tracking some students towards college and others for a career, then that era is over. The time has truly come for a paradigm change. The idea that a university degree is for everyone straight out of high school is gone. The notion that our students will pick a career and stick with the same company for 40 years, retiring with a gold watch, is obsolete. The notion of career and college readiness must truly embrace both sides. Our world has changed and so must our perspective.

We need to guide our students to careers rather than just to college. We need to help them see the many pathways from internships to industry certifications to military to university that can help them achieve their goal of being gainfully and happily employed. It is our job to help them realize that skills are now more important than the piece of paper one frames on the wall.

As an educator and/or as a parent, you have the chance to help other make great choices. You can involve today's youth in both looking at their skills and competencies, as well as their personalities. Once your students know themselves, you can help them explore careers that would be a good fit until they are ready to set a tentative career goal. From there, your guidance will be needed to help them research different paths as they establish their skill-based educational plan.

All of this is within your realm. It will take more time than giving everyone the same spiel about going to a 4-year university program, but it will be well worth it. It is your job - our job - to help all our students be prepared for their future. We must advise students based on the realities of the labor market and promote CTE as an equally viable path to success.

Remember that the goal is not high school graduation. It is not just entrance into college. The goal is not even university graduation. At least it shouldn't be. The true goal is to prepare for a career that can support one's family in today's economy and to ensure our students are satisfied as they contribute to their local community. That plan may include the university...or it may include a different albeit equally viable path. I believe we need to redefine the goal of our educational system from simply being a graduate, to becoming career-ready.

There is an often-confusing mix of definitions, frameworks, policies and implementation strategies for career readiness. Some viewpoints center on learning skills for a specific entry-level job, while others define career readiness as a broader understanding of workplace skills. Still other definitions focus on knowledge and skills for a particular industry sector such as health sciences or marketing. Career readiness is a convergence of all of these definitions. The definition I particularly like the best is from a broad-based coalition of education, policy, business, and philanthropic organizations called the Career Readiness Partner Council.[1] They define the goal as follows:

> *A career-ready person effectively navigates pathways that connect education and employment to achieve a fulfilling, financially-secure and successful career. A career is more than just a job. Career readiness has no defined endpoint. To be career ready in our ever-changing global economy requires adaptability and a commitment to lifelong learning, along with mastery of key academic, technical and workplace knowledge, skills and dispositions that vary from one career to another and change over time as a person progresses along a developmental continuum. Knowledge, skills and dispositions that are inter-dependent and mutually reinforcing.*

I have adopted this definition and invite you to do the same.

Time to fly

I would equate what we're doing to an airplane that's just taking off. It's interesting to me because runways at the airport are designed to face a particular orientation. They always build runways to face into the wind, so that a plane faces the wind when taking off. It never made sense to me because I always thought the wind should be behind the plane to help the plane go faster to help take off. But in fact, the aerodynamics work in such a way that it is more helpful for the wind to be beating against the front of the plane as it gains speed on the runway. The key for the plane is to never stop, never slow down and never quit, but to pick up more speed and press against the wind until soon the wind that's coming against it moves under it, allowing for lift to take place, allowing the plane to fly.

I share this because I know you will put down this book and return to your various campuses. As we arrive with new ideas and perhaps a new perspective, as we are on our local roadways, there will be many different winds blowing against us. Sometimes those winds are people who are working in our own institution. Sometimes those winds are our spouses who ask, "Why do you work so hard?" Sometimes those winds are our fellow teachers and administrators, contently complacent. Sometimes those winds are how we feel, unappreciated in what it is that we are doing. I am telling you that no matter what those winds are, the same laws of aerodynamics can work for us: Do not stop. Do not slow down. Do not quit. We need professionals like you who have open minds, who have a good vision, and who have heart; we need you active and engaged for the benefit of every student. I invite you, in spite of the winds that are coming against us, let's all pick up even more speed. My promise is that the same things that are against us today will be same things that are under us tomorrow, allowing us to fly to great heights.

Remain focused on the ultimate goal for our students. The goal is not just high school graduation. It is not merely entrance into college. The ultimate goal is not even solely university graduation. The true goal is to prepare today's students for a career that can support their family in tomorrow's economy and to ensure our students are satisfied as they contribute to their local community.

I invite you to help me in (re)defining the goal of our educational system to creating career-ready individuals. Join the thousands of other educators and parents in America that are embracing the genius of the AND. By changing both the advice that we give and the questions we ask, we will adapt to fit the new rules of the game.

All students deserve the opportunity to truly be career-ready upon completing their education. Our student's future is contingent upon our success. Let's not let them down.

It's time to fly.

———

ALSO BY KEVIN J FLEMING

Maintaining Strategic Relevance: Career & Technical Education Program Discontinuance in Community and Technical Colleges

Success in The New Economy: How All Students Can Gain a Competitive Advantage (animated video)

Introduction to the Automated Warehouse (free eTextbook)

APPENDIX A

OVERVIEW FOR PARENT/ GUARDIAN'S GUIDE TO ENSURING YOUR STUDENT'S SUCCESS

I decided to include a guide to help parents understand the process that you will go through with your students. Most parents want to help their children succeed and many would be willing to work with their children if they only knew what to do. However, most parents do not understand what can be done or how instrumental they are to their child's decision-making process when it comes to careers.

The following guide is a quick summary of this book written specifically to the parent. Many sentences are word for word from the main book. The purpose is to outline why skills assessment, personality review, and career exploration are necessary. It also explains why a 4-year college education isn't what it used to be. The hope is that it will help parents change their paradigm about post-secondary education and help them help their child through the career-choosing maze.

You can use this guide in many ways. First, you can simply copy it and hand it to parents. Though this may be tempting, it may not be the best way to go. I suggest that you at least meet with parents and give them an overall explanation.

The second use is to provide the information to parents section by section, perhaps over a series of parent workshops. Once again, meeting with parents to explain the next step would be very useful.

Thirdly, you can use this guide as an outline for presentations to parents, either individually or in groups. Afterward, you might want to offer them either the entire guide to take home or the needed links.

A final potential use is to purchase copies of this book for all your parents and flag this appendix for them. Encourage them to read this section first; then they can go back and read previous sections in more detail.

Remember, parents can be the key to helping your students figure out their career path. Help your students by making their parents your allies.

A Parent/Guardian's Guide to Ensuring your Student's Success

Introduction

The intent of this guide is not to tell you or your child what to do. What your child does after high school is a decision you both need to make together. This guide is written to tell you the truth about today's labor market and what the new rules are so that you can make the best decisions possible and be better consumers of higher education.

I'm going to share with you some facts that you may not have ever heard, give you some ideas to consider, and outline six key strategies on how to best support your child so they can be as successful as possible after high school.

The "One Way to Win" Lie

Education is core to your child's success. But, in order to help them navigate education beyond high school, you must understand the current misalignment between education and our workforce. Tables like the one below are used to show parents and students that there is a correlation between higher degrees and higher income.[2] It shows that, on average, a person with a university degree earns far more money than the average person without a high school diploma.

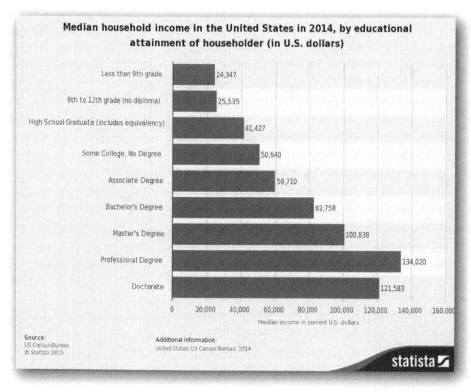

Median household income in the United States in 2014, by educational attainment of householder (in U.S. dollars)

Statistics show that Associate Degree earners range between $27,000-$72,000 while Bachelor's recipients earn between $35,000 - $100,000. But this data only accounts for the 25th to the 75th percentile of adult workers. This means 25% of Associate Degree holders earn more than $72,000 annually, and 25% of Bachelor's degree holders earn less than $35,000 per year – something the charts do not show.[3]

This idea that 4-year college degrees always have higher earnings has fueled a "college for all" philosophy. It has caused parents to encourage their children to go to the university – any university – to major in anything – in pursuit of future job security, social mobility, and financial prosperity.

This philosophy has increased college enrollment, resulting in 66 percent of high school graduates enrolling in higher education right after high school.[4] Initially, they are deemed the successful ones. But, what you won't see advertised is the reality that most drop out. Nationally, only about half of those enrolling in a four-year university will actually graduate.[5] Many students are not adequately prepared, occupationally focused, or emotionally equipped to succeed.

Since most students are told a university degree guarantees a higher salary, they often delay their career planning until after high school. Some even wait until after college graduation. The problem is that not every degree is direct preparation for employment. With rising education costs, a shrinking job market, and the over-saturation of some academic majors in the workforce, many students end up taking positions that do not require the education they have received, at a financial cost that is more than they can afford.

The Economic Reality

Our world has changed. In 1960, when taking into account all jobs in the economy, 20% were professional jobs requiring a 4-year degree or higher, 20% of all jobs were technical jobs requiring skilled training, and 60% were classified as unskilled.[6] Fast forward to 2018. Harvard University projects only 33% of all jobs will require a 4-year degree or more, 30% will require a technical certificate or Associate's degree, and 36% will require a high school diploma with a certification or on-the-job-training.[7] So, while most

jobs in the future will require some education and training beyond high school, the majority of occupations will not require a Bachelor's degree.

That 4-year degree may offer benefits such as increased civic engagement and intellectual enlightenment, but does it guarantee employment? Think about people you know who, from an economic perspective, inefficiently spent time and money to get a degree that perhaps they didn't really need for their career. It may be hard initially to accept, but a university degree is no longer the guaranteed path to economic success, as it was for prior generations.

The true ratio of jobs in our economy is 1:2:7.[8] For every occupation that requires a master's degree or more, two professional jobs require a university degree, and there are over half a dozen jobs requiring a 1-year certificate or 2-year degree. Each of these technicians is in very high-skilled areas that are in great demand. This ratio is fundamental to all industries. It was the same in 1960, and will be the same in 2030.

Unlike two generations ago, having hands-on skills and perfecting what your child is good at can be more valuable in today's economy than getting a degree in 'something' simply to get one. In fact, a recent Gallup-Lumina Poll[9] found that when hiring, business leaders indicated that the candidate's school and college major had less to do with employment than a candidate's skills and knowledge in a specific field.

Formal education does count and many students now secure degrees, but few have employable skills. In tomorrow's economy, skills count more than degrees. Fortunately, students no longer need to decide between college readiness or career preparation. It's possible, and increasingly necessary, to achieve both. Understanding this reality is how you can help your children benefit from their education and best prepare them for their future.

The time has come to redefine the goal for our children. Is the goal simply high school graduation, or just to graduate with a college degree? Or is the ultimate goal a well-paying career where they are fulfilled? If it is the latter, a 4-year university degree may or may not be the best option for them right after high school.

Parents, guardians, counselors, and teachers must emphasize that there are multiple pathways to career success. The secret is to align your child's initial career choice with their skills and abilities.

Is My Help Really Necessary?

Yes! Parents are the most important resource a child can have when it comes to career exploration after their own interests. Studies have shown that parents have the greatest influence on their child's career choices.[10] Not only that, but you know your child intimately. Who else would be better prepared to help them learn about themselves, their likes and dislikes, and their talents?

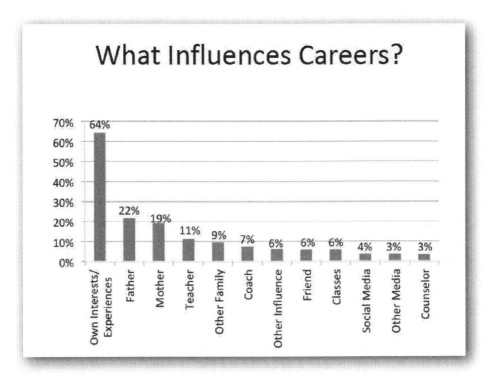

Finding the right career rarely just happens, at least not the first time. For those without a plan, years can be spent fumbling from one job to another before something finally fits. Careful planning in the early years can stop this terrible waste of time and money. As a parent, you have the ability to help your child create a plan that will offer them the best hope of success.

When you can identify those careers which fit who they are, regardless if it is a surgeon, dental assistant, business manager, or electrician, then the money will flow and your child will be happy in the process. That's how you use the realities of the labor market to position your child for high-wage, in-demand jobs.

Keep in mind that career exploration is truly exploration. There is no need to set anything in stone. Learning about different career paths will help your child focus on career possibilities, thus making their schooling more relevant.

But how do you know what they are good at, what kind of personality they have and what jobs are out there that fit? To prepare your child for career success, and long before they enroll in college classes, help your child focus on six steps: Self-Exploration, Personality Assessment, Career Exploration, Setting a Tentative Career Goal, Education/Training Research, and Establishing a Skills-Based Educational Plan.

Step One: Self-Exploration

Naturally, you can also ask your child questions about their likes and dislikes. For instance, what is their favorite subject? What activities do they enjoy doing alone or with friends? What things do they find interesting?

In addition to asking questions, look at what you see them doing in their free time. What are their hobbies? What clubs are the involved in? What television shows or books does your child enjoy? What kinds of things capture their attention when surfing the web?

Finally, find out what your child sees as their ideal life. How would they like to live, spend their time, with whom, and what would they want to learn? This can be done as a game – what if your life could be anything, what would it be? Don't focus on jobs, but on lifestyles.

Now it is time to ask three very important questions. I encourage you to have this conversation with them to begin the career exploration process.

1. What do you enjoy doing?
2. What are you good at doing?
3. What can you get paid to do?

These might sound very similar, but these are three very different questions. For example, I love to sing, and I'm fairly good at it, too. I can carry a tune and sang in my college choir, but I don't think anyone will pay to hear me sing. That makes singing a good hobby, but not a viable career option for me.

On the other hand, I have Type A personality which means I like everything to be organized and neat. As a result, I am very good at organizing and cleaning the house. I'm certain that I could get people to pay me to clean their house, but I don't like doing it. Therefore, cleaning would make a good occupation, but not for me since I don't enjoy the work.

For me, cleaning would be a good "Plan B." A "Plan B" occupation could be something that your child could fall back on if they needed to – or it could make for a good part-time job while in school.

If your teen has the same answer to all three questions, then that could be their dream job. For example, they may love to build things, be good at building things, and be able to get paid well as a Construction Manager in your region. Perhaps they love to work with animals, are good at working with animals, and are able to get paid well as a Veterinarian Technician.

Once you and your child have begun to identify interests, find ways to develop those interests to see where it may lead. Consider joining 4-H or scouting, get a part-time job in an area that is of interest, take an online class in something like website design, volunteer, do service that requires the use of certain skills, find toys that require specific skill sets such as building robotics, join a team, or a myriad of other things available in your community.

Here are a few good free resources for self-exploration:

Career InfoNet Skills Profiler: This allows your child to choose from seven different skill groups including basic skills, social skills, complex problem-solving skills, technical skills, system skills, resource management skills, and desktop computer skills. http://www.careerinfonet.org/skills/skills_list.aspx

Career Values Scale: These 88 questions look at your child's values and see how they relate to work. This will help your child determine the level of satisfaction they will derive from different careers. http://quintcareers.testingroom.com/

Work Preference Inventory: Twenty-four questions will assess your child's work style. http://www.careerperfect.com/services/free/work-preference/

Also, both the California CareerZone (https://www.cacareerzone.org/guide/parents) and the California Career Center (https://www.calcareercenter.org/Home/Content?categoryID=89) have resources to help parents/guardians use these sites with their students. Not many other identified resources have explicit parent/guardian aids.

Step Two: Personality Assessment

Beyond skills is the personality of your child. Studies have shown that people find a career the most satisfying when it fits with their own style of operation. Learning about their personality traits, personal qualities, and work environment preferences will help your child understand what motivates them and brings them the most satisfaction. This will help them make career and educational choices that suit who they are.

Some free personality tests to consider are:

Myers-Briggs Type Indicator (MBTI): This personality test is one of the most trusted. It has been selected by the nation's top colleges to help with career development and is backed by scientific research.[11] This test will help your child understand themselves and how they interact with others. It will help them identify their preferences in four areas: where they focus their attention, how they take in information, how they make decisions based on the information, and how they deal with the world. The original test costs $49.95, however, a free version can be found at http://www.truity.com/test/type-finder-research-edition.

ColorCode: Identifies driving core motives, helping your child understand why they do what they do. https://www.color-code.com/free_personality_test/

Step Three: Career Exploration

They say that today's high school seniors will have an average of 10-14 jobs by their 40th birthday.[12] The era of receiving a golden watch for a lifetime of service to a single company is gone. This means that every child in middle and high school needs the opportunity to explore and experiment with various careers and industries.

Whether your child completes high school, enters the workforce, or matriculates to college, all students need to understand and explore different career possibilities. The sooner they do this, the better.

One challenge to a successful career exploration approach is the sheer magnitude of jobs that exist today. According to the Department of Labor, there are nearly 1,000 different occupational titles in existence.[13] That's a lot of occupations to explore. If your student chose one per day, it would take three years to explore all the jobs! Fortunately, the U.S. Department of Education developed the career pathway model to make this process easier to navigate.

Sixteen (16) industry clusters have been endorsed by the federal government as a mechanism for showing students potential career pathways within any field of interest. Many states tweaked them (California has 15 and Hawaii has 6), but the principle remains the same. The 16 include:[14]

- Agriculture, Food, and Natural Resources
- Architecture and Construction
- Arts, Audio/Video Technology, and Communications

- Business, Management, and Administration
- Education and Training
- Finance
- Government and Public Administration
- Health Science
- Hospitality and Tourism
- Human Services
- Information Technology
- Law, Public Safety, Corrections, and Security
- Manufacturing
- Marketing, Sales, and Service
- Science, Technology, Engineering, and Mathematics
- Transportation, Distribution, and Logistics

The point of career exploration is all about understanding the jobs available, the income ranges they pay, and evaluating the skills they require. For your child to make productive career decisions, they must explore and investigate many occupations. Often, a child's knowledge of careers is limited to what they see on television or what their family members do for a living.[15] One of the best strategies is active participation in career technical education classes and extended learning opportunities.

Participation in a career technical student organizations provides the opportunity for both career exploration and the acquisition of employability skills which most employers value.[16] Employability skills are necessary for getting, keeping and being successful in a career pathway – and they are transferable between different industries.[17] Gaining these skills early gives your student a competitive advantage after graduation.

Another thing you can do is start talking to your child about how their current interests relate to careers. For example, if your child loves to draw, talk about different careers that use drawing such as designing homes, creating magazine ads, and drawing cartoons. Continue the idea of art by talking about photography, flower arranging, or cake decorating.

Whether your child's skills lie in art or something else like being social, being outdoors, helping others, or math and science, try to find examples of real life situations where they could use those skills and be paid to do so. The key is to help them see a connection between what they enjoy doing and possible occupations associated with these interests.

At this time, investigation should not be limited. Help your child check out several career options that match their interests, as well as how they wish to work. This will help them be more realistic about future plans. When looking at a career possibility, do more than check out the everyday tasks involved. Be sure to look at the following as well:

- Education needed and how the education/training/skills can be obtained
- The outlook for this career – is it growing?
- The advancement possibilities
- Any benefits such as health care, retirement, travel, etc.
- Typical wages
- Where these jobs are located

Please do not stop at researching jobs. Do everything you can to allow your child to experience careers as well. You can do this by having your child:

- Interview people in a field they are considering. Ask them all the questions above as well as why they like what they do and what they don't like about what they do.
- Go to career fairs
- Ask someone if your child can shadow them on the job for a few days.
- Participate in an internship
- Participate in work-based learning
- Volunteer
- Take CTE classes
- Go on field trips

Luckily, there are many good resources available for career exploration. Some schools have a career center. If this is the case for you, then that would be a great place to start. Also, some local libraries have career systems in place. If not, though, do not despair because there are other options.

The Internet is full of reliable websites that help you learn about careers and career exploration. Don't be afraid to explore sites designed by specific states even if you live elsewhere. Often, a majority of the information will be pertinent regardless of where you live.

Here are some good free tests that can help guide a student towards careers based on their interests and skills:

Career Interest Profiler: 180-question assessment measures occupation and career interests. http://quintcareers.testingroom. com/

Holland Code Career Test: Helps your child identify career interest among six themes: realistic, investigative, artistic, social, enterprising, and conventional. Offers a list of suggested careers based on the profile. http://www.truity.com/test/ holland-code-career-test

Here are other sites that can guide you through the entire career maze. Although made and named for California, they are free to everyone:

California Career Café: Created for community college students, this site is free and useful to high school students as well. It helps them identify their strengths, talents, interests and educational options. It also helps students explore careers, connect them to employers, and teach them what soft skills are needed by these employers. http://www.cacareercafe.com/

California Career Center: This is a career planning website helping your child create a Career Action Plan that includes identification of multiple goals. It will help them develop career self-management skills. https://www.calcareercenter.org/

DreamCatcher: Helps students identify their purpose in life and achieve their career dreams through eight interactive lessons. Each module is independent and can be taught as standalone units, and can be easily integrated into any classroom, after school group, or home schooling curriculum. www.TelosES.com

The point to this exploration is to help your child find career possibilities of interest. Be sure that you are not steering your child towards something because it would be of interest to you. Also, be sure to be supportive as career interests grow, develop, and change. The more information your child has, the better able they will be to make a final decision that meets their needs.

Step Four: Set a Tentative Career Goal

After your child has spent time researching themselves and potential careers, it is time to pick a tentative career goal. Be sure that your child understands that this goal is for a first career and that it is only tentative. If, after more exploration, they want to make a change, it will be much easier because they already have done steps 1 through 3.

It is important for your child to set a flexible career goal based on their personality and abilities, and not just their interests. This career goal may not be what they'll want to do for the rest of their life. It's helping them make a primary Plan A and a back-up Plan B so they are prepared to pivot in response to life's many uncertainties, such as the changing job market and emerging career opportunities. This is especially true if your child is entrepreneurial. 63% of twenty-somethings want to be their own boss...and creating good jobs while rebuilding America's middle-class hinges on the success of small businesses and startups.[18]

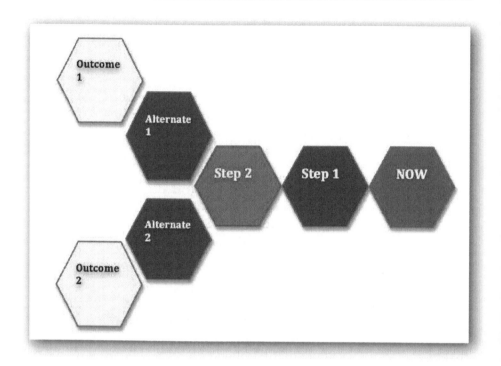

Step Five: Education/Training Research

Once your child has a career in mind, it is time to research what it takes to become what they wish to become. For many occupations, there are many paths, so be sure to invite your child to explore all available options.

This is going to require some out of the box thinking. Don't get stuck in the "4-year university for everyone" rut. There are many options available, many of which do not require a 4-year degree. Some of these include:

1. Career and Technical Education (CTE)
2. Bachelor's Degree
3. Bachelor's Degree in Technology
4. 2-year Associates Degree
5. 1-year technical certificates
6. Regional Occupation Program (ROP)
7. Military Service
8. Online Education

9. A year studying abroad
10. A prep/gap year
11. Private Career Schools and Colleges
12. Full-time Employment
13. Formal Apprenticeships/Internships
14. Religious Missionary Service
15. Peace Corps or other International Volunteer Program
16. Americorps or other National Service Program
17. Volunteer Work
18. Adult Schools

For instance, if your child wants to be an interior designer, they will find that there are certificate programs, 2-year associate programs, and 4-year programs available. When it comes to certifications, there are core, advanced, and specialty courses available. Additionally, your child may want to think about an internship or apprenticeship.[19]

Finally, while in high school, they may want to consider getting a job that uses interior design skills such as merchandise display, wallpaper hanger, or painter. If they can't find work with an interior designer, they could look for work in similar fields such as architecture or floral design.

They will also want to consider high school classes that give them the types of skills needed to be an interior designer such as a communications class that will teach them to convey oral information effectively, classes that help them with critical thinking, and geometry classes that teach them how much paint or wallpaper to order based on the area of the wall to be covered.

Step Six: Establish a Skill-Based Educational Plan

Now that your child has several education pathways that have been researched, they need to choose the one that best suits them. Your child's education plan should be primarily informed by their self-awareness of strengths and a tentative career goal. They will consider their interest in more schooling, the cost of schooling, the location of training, the amount of money they will make with additional training, the ability to get training while working, along with many other factors.

This plan will be the blueprint for what classes they take in high school, the post-secondary programs they wish to complete, and the institutions they apply to attend. Because of this plan, your child will see the reason behind the courses they take and find true relevance to their coursework. It is important that this plan also includes the specific skills and certificates they will need to enter their first chosen career.

Not every set of knowledge can be gained inside a classroom. In addition to the classes and degrees required, a Skill-Based Education Plan should also include the skills, competencies, licenses, and experiences your child should secure before attempting to secure gainful employment. Consider informational interviews with particular individuals in the field, industry books that should be read, technical certifications (e.g. CISCO) that should be earned, and conferences/events/experiences that should be part of their plan. For example, participating in Habitat for Humanity building a house would be a great experience if their goal is engineering, construction, or architecture.

Two of the best ways to create a Skills-Based Education Plan are:

1. <u>DreamCatcher</u>: Identify your purpose in life and achieve your career dreams through eight interactive lessons. Each lesson is interactive with great videos and an online tool to talk to other students with similar career interests. www.TelosES.com
2. <u>California Career Center</u>: This is a career planning website to help you create an education plan with many different options. It will also help you develop career self-management skills. https://www.calcareercenter.org/

If you homeschool, also check out www.My10YearPlan.com for an in-depth curriculum for students to develop a quantitative and meaningful 10-year career, education, and life plan and portfolio.

The time has come to redefine the goal for our children. Is the goal simply high school graduation or just to graduate with a college degree? Or is the ultimate goal a well-paying career where they are fulfilled?

Ultimately, your child's first career choice is a personal decision, and it may change many times. Everyone wants what is best for their child, but it is important to be careful not to steer them to a particular career that we think is best for them. As an involved parent, the key to your child's success is to provide ample opportunities to explore and develop their interests and abilities through a variety of career and technical education coursework and out-of-class clubs/experiences.

Continue to encourage them to gain technical skills, academic knowledge, life skills, and employability skills. This is how you can help your children apply their education and best prepare them for their future.

1 http://www.careerreadynow.org

2 United States; US Census Bureau; 2014, http://www.statista.com/statistics/233301/median-household-income-in-the-united-states-by-education/

3 U.S. Census Bureau, 2012, Table PINC-03; U.S. Census Bureau, 2012a

4 U.S. Department of Education, National Center for Education Statistics. (2015). The Condition of Education 2015 (NCES 2015-144), Immediate College Enrollment Rate.

5 U.S. Department of Education, National Center for Education Statistics. (2015). The Condition of Education 2015 (NCES 2015-144), Institutional Retention and Graduation Rates for Undergraduate Students.

6 Project Lead the Way (www.pltw.org). And: GetReal (www.getrealca.com).

7 90% of all jobs in the future will require some education and training beyond high school according to: The National Science Foundation (2012) PI Conference keynote by Jane Oates, Assistant Secretary ETA, Department of Labor. And: Symonds, W., Schwartz, R., & Ferguson, R. (February 2011). *Pathways to Prosperity: Meeting the Challenge of Preparing Young Americans for the 21st Century*. Report issued by the Pathways to Prosperity Project, Harvard Graduate School of Education. And: Deil-Amen & DeLuca. (2010). *The Underserved Third: How our Educational Structures Populate an Educational Underclass*. Routledge. And: The Bureau of Labor Statistics, Occupational Outlook Handbook, 2010-2011 Edition. And: The Workforce Alliance. (2009). *California's Forgotten Middle-Skill Jobs: Meeting the Demands of a 21st Century Economy*. Washington DC.

8 Gray, K. & Herr, E. (2006). *Other Ways to Win: Creating Alternatives for High School Graduates*. *Third Edition*. Thousand Oaks: Corwin Press.

9 http://www.gallup.com/poll/167546/business-leaders-say-knowledge-trumps-college-pedigree.aspx

10 Pezirkianidis, Christos, Christina Athanasiades, and Natalia Moutopoulou. "The relationship between adolescents' perception of their parents' jobs and their future career orientation." Scientific Annals-School of Psychology 10 (2013): 100-126.

11 https://www.cpp.com/products/mbti/index.aspx

12 http://futureworkplace.com/wp-content/uploads/MultipleGenAtWork_infographic.pdf

13 "Bureau of Labor Statistics, U.S. Department of Labor, 2014–2015 Occupational Outlook Handbook, [date accessed] [http://www.bls.gov/ooh/]."

14 https://www.onetonline.org/find/career?c=0&g=Go

15 Michigan State University. "Parents still major influence on child's decision to pursue science careers." ScienceDaily. ScienceDaily, 21 February 2010. <www.sciencedaily.com/releases/2010/02/100220204814.htm>.

16 http://cte.ed.gov/employabilityskills/

17 www.skillsyouneed.com

18 http://www.phoenix.edu/news/releases/2015/08/uopx_workplace_survey_finds_more_than_one_third_working_adults_consider_themselves_intrapreneurs.html

19 http://www.onetonline.org/link/summary/27-1025.00

APPENDIX B

Overview for Guide for Students to Gain a Competitive Advantage

I have also included here a guide for students that they can read and navigate on their own. If you have students that are self-motivated, then it might be helpful to give them the information found in the following pages.

Once again, the guide is a quick summary of this book written specifically to the student. The information is not new but is geared towards a student who is wondering what to do next. It outlines specific skills they will need as adults, as well as the need for exploration of self and careers. It also helps them see that there are many paths to success that do not all include a 4-year college degree. Instead of being broken into 6 steps, the student guide is broken into 4 steps for easier consumption.

As with the parent's guide, you can use this guide in similar ways. If you give it to a student, I suggest you do so with some guiding words and support. However, since you have the opportunity to meet with your students regularly, you may want to consider giving them a section at a time with some kind of assignment or homework resulting in a guided and collaborative exploration process.

Finally, you can use this guide as an outline for presentations to students, either individually or in groups. Afterward, you might want to offer them either the entire guide to take home or the needed links.

Note that I also developed an animated companion video entitled, "4 Skills & 4 Steps" which is posted on YouTube.com. It serves as a great introduction to this material with your student(s).

Getting your students on board with this process is key to helping them find the career path of their choice. This guide is a good way to facilitate the conversation and help them in achieving their dreams.

———

A Guide for Students to Gain a Competitive Advantage

The Four Kinds of Skills You Need

In this guide, we are going to talk about preparing for life after high school. This includes getting a job, finding a career, and earning a living. In order to prepare for success, first we must define it.

The American workforce has changed a lot recently. Occupations in every industry now require a combination of both academic knowledge and technical skills. If you don't have both, you will have trouble finding a job. If you do have both, you will be more employable.

This means that you need to graduate from high school ready for both college and careers. To do this, you'll need to develop skills in four specific areas to achieve your dreams.

The first set of skills you need to master are ***academic skills***. The classes you are taking matter in the world of work. However, getting good grades isn't the whole picture. Understanding how to apply the knowledge to real-world problems is also important. This will help you be competitive when you graduate, giving you more options to choose from.

You can also earn college credit now while still in school. This can be done through articulation, dual enrollment, and/or concurrent enrollment.

The point is to really take your classes seriously. Work to be the strongest reader, writer, and thinker you can be.

The second area are _**life skills**_. These skills are about everyday real world survival. They include things like how to bounce back after a bad experience, how to manage money and create a family budget, and how to remain healthy through good nutrition. Some of the keys to success are perseverance, grit, knowing how to set goals, and identifying a plan of action for your future. Life skills will give you a strong foundation for fulfilling your true potential.

Local employers also expect certain things of people they hire. These are called _**employability skills**_ and make up the third set of skills you should focus on. In fact, people who get the best jobs and keep them have this nailed. Employers expect you to have these skills from your very first day on the job. You may not realize it, but your teachers are working hard at giving you employability skills. Think of the deadlines you are given, the teams you work in, and the projects you organize. Learning how to manage your time, creatively solve problems, and communicate appropriately will help prepare you for the world of work.

Finally, there are _**technical skills**_. These can be very industry-specific. They include the ability to apply what you have learned to working a computer, running a machine, or monitoring a patient's heart rate. High school students that are savvy with skills in areas of interest to them will find jobs, keep them, and get promoted more quickly. You should definitely find ways to earn certificates and industry credentials in technical fields on your way to graduation.

Local employers will want to know what you can do, and what you can do well, not just what diploma hangs on your wall. In fact, with or without a 4-year degree, technical skills are the new currency in today's world.

Making Your Skills Count

Success depends on aligning your career with your skills and available job opportunities. In today's world, having marketable skills and perfecting what you are good at is more valuable than getting a degree in 'something' simply to get one. With a shrinking middle class, a 4-year degree is no longer a guaranteed path towards financial success. [1]

A 4-year degree may make you well educated, but not every degree is direct preparation for employment. This misalignment between degrees and job skills causes half of university graduates to be under-employed in what are called gray-collar jobs where they take positions that do not require the education they have received, often with debt they can't afford.

More than likely, you've seen a graph something like this that shows you that getting a degree is the right way to go.[2]

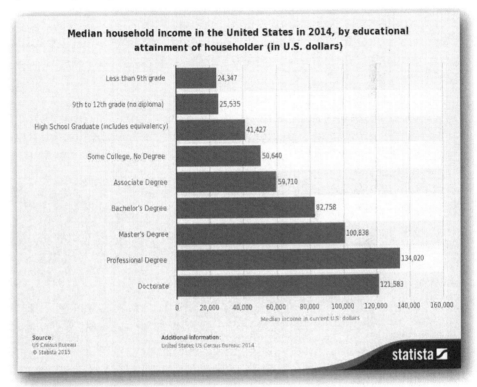

But this is not the whole truth. Let's say you were considering a career as either an electrician or a business manager. You would find that the average annual income for electricians is $51,000, only about half of the $105,000 average wage for management occupations.[3] So, at first glance it looks as if getting a bachelor's degree in business is a no-brainer, but adding skills and ability into the picture adds a whole new dynamic.

What if you have the potential to become an excellent electrician, but lack the skills and ability to be an excellent manager? Then you should be looking at projected incomes towards the bottom of the pay scale for managers and towards the top for electricians. You would then discover that electricians near the top of the pay scale make around $86,000, which is far higher than the income of a manager near the bottom of the pay scale at $52,000.[4]

Now, this is just one example, but the concept is true throughout all industries. The claim that you will make more money with an increased amount of education is not necessarily inaccurate, it's just incomplete. That advice is based on the averages, but no one is perfectly average.

Everyone has a unique blend of skills, talents, and interests.

Remember that graduating from high school is just the first step. It is necessary to continue to pursue more learning. A majority of positions that pay good wages require skills associated with at least some education beyond high school. Yet, there is growing evidence of a skills gap in which many young Americans are not receiving the hands-on training that is needed.

Our president in his state of the union speech said, "I ask every American to commit to at least one year or more of higher education or career training… whatever the training may be…every American will need to get more than a high school diploma."[5]

You see, while many of us want to be the boss, this isn't what is always needed in today's world of work. Because the true ratio of jobs in our economy is 1:2:7.[6] For every occupation that requires a master's degree or more, two professional jobs require a university degree, and there are over half a dozen jobs requiring a 1-year certificate or 2-year Associates degree from a community/technical college...and each of these technicians is in very high-skilled areas that are in great demand! This ratio is true for all industries. It was the same in 1950, the same in 1990, and will be the same in 2030.

And this is part of the reason why about four out of every five graduates with a 2-year associate degree or less have the same annual income as those with a 4-year college degree.[7] In the new economy, skills are actually just as important as a degree, and many careers available will require the mastery of hands-on technical skills.

———

Now, you're probably wondering what you need to do to accomplish your dreams. So, how about some advice? Here are four steps you can take to figure out what job best suits you and how to get it.

Step 1: Learn About Yourself and Your Talents

This step begins with taking assessments that help identify your talents, values, interests, skills, and strengths. This first step will help you identify academic and career options that align with who you are and with your natural abilities.

Here are a few good free resources for self-exploration:

California Career Zone: A career exploration and planning system designed just for students! This site has information on over 900 occupations. It has many easy to use assessments, as well as career videos, and job openings. https://www.cacareerzone.org
Work Preference Inventory: Twenty-four questions will assess your work style. http://www.careerperfect.com/services/free/work-preference/

You also need to think about your likes and dislikes. What is your favorite subject? What do you enjoy doing alone or with friends? What do you find interesting? What are your hobbies? What clubs are you involved in?

What TV shows or books do you enjoy? What do you enjoying looking at when surfing the web?

Finally, consider what you see in your ideal life. Write a few paragraphs that answer how you would like to live, spend your time, with whom, and what you would want to learn. Essentially, what if your life could be anything, what would it be? Don't focus on jobs, but on lifestyles.

Now it is time to ask yourself three very important questions.

1. What do I enjoy doing?
2. What am I good at doing?
3. What can I get paid to do?

These might sound very similar, but these are three very different questions. For example, I love to sing, and I'm fairly good at it, too. I can carry a tune and sang in my college choir, but I don't think anyone will pay to hear me sing. That makes singing a good hobby, but not a viable career option for me.

On the other hand, I have Type A personality which means I like everything to be organized and neat. As a result, I am very good at organizing and cleaning the house. I'm certain that I could get people to pay me to clean their house, but I don't like doing it. Therefore, cleaning would make a good occupation, but not for me since I don't enjoy the work.

For me, cleaning would be a good "Plan B." A "Plan B" occupation could be something that you could fall back on if you needed to – or it could make for a good part-time job while in school.

If you have the same answer to all three questions, then this could be your dream job. For example, you may love to build things, be good at building things, and be able to get paid well as a Construction Manager in your region. Perhaps you love to work with animals, are good at working with animals, and are able to get paid well as a Veterinarian Technician.

Beyond just skills, you need to consider your personality. Studies have shown that most people find a career the most satisfying when it fits with their own style of operation. Learning about your personality traits, personal qualities, and work environment preferences will help you understand what motivates you and brings you the most satisfaction. This will help you make career and educational choices that suit who you are.

Some free personality tests to consider are:

ColorCode: Identifies driving core motives, helping you understand why you do what you do. https://www.colorcode.com/free_personality_test/

Myers-Briggs Type Indicator (MBTI): This personality test is one of the most trusted. It has been selected by the nation's top colleges to help with career development and is backed by scientific research. This assessment will help you understand yourself and how you interact with others. It will help you identify your preferences in four areas: where you focus your attention, how you take in information, how you make decisions based on the information, and how you deal with the world. The original test costs $49.95, however, a free version can be found at http://www.truity.com/test/type-finder-research-edition.

Once you have begun to identify interests and your personality, find ways to develop those interests to see where it may lead. Consider joining 4-H or scouting, get a part-time job in an area that is of interest, take an online class in something like website design, volunteer, do service that requires the use of certain skills, join a team, or a myriad of other things available in your community.

Step 2: Explore All Possible Career Options

They say that you are likely to have an average of 10 to 14 jobs in your lifetime.[8] The era of receiving a golden watch for a lifetime of service to a single company, as your grandparents did, is long gone. This means that you must take the opportunity to explore and experiment with various careers and industries.

Whether you complete high school, enter the workforce, or matriculate to college, you will need to understand and explore different career possibilities. The sooner you do this, the better.

One challenge to a successful career exploration approach is the sheer magnitude of jobs that exist today. According to the Department of Labor, there are nearly 1,000 different occupational titles in existence.[9] That's a lot of occupations to explore. If you chose one per day, it would take three years to explore all the jobs! Fortunately, the U.S. Department of Education has endorsed the career pathway model to make this process easier to navigate.

Sixteen (16) industry clusters were developed as a mechanism for showing students potential career pathways within any field of interest. These include:[10]

- Agriculture, Food, and Natural Resources
- Architecture and Construction
- Arts, Audio/Video Technology, and Communications
- Business, Management, and Administration
- Education and Training
- Finance
- Government and Public Administration
- Health Science
- Hospitality and Tourism
- Human Services
- Information Technology
- Law, Public Safety, Corrections, and Security
- Manufacturing
- Marketing, Sales, and Service
- Science, Technology, Engineering, and Mathematics
- Transportation, Distribution, and Logistics

The point of career exploration is all about understanding the jobs available, the income ranges they pay, and evaluating the skills they require. For you to make productive career decisions, you must explore and investigate many occupations.

Be honest. How many careers do you really know about? Your knowledge is probably limited to what you've seen online or what family members do for a living.[11] But there is so much more available to you. One of the best strategies to learn more is through active participation in career technical education classes and extended learning opportunities.

At this time, investigation should not be limited. Check out several career options that match your interests, as well as how you wish to work. This will help you be more realistic about future plans. When looking at a career possibility, do more than check out the everyday tasks involved. Be sure to look at the following as well:

- Education needed and where the education can be obtained
- The outlook for this career – is it growing?
- The advancement possibilities
- Any benefits such as health care, retirement, travel, etc
- Typical wages
- Where these jobs are located

Please do not stop at researching jobs. Do everything you can to experience careers as well. You can do this by:

- Interviewing people in a field you are considering. Ask them all the questions above as well as why they like what they do and what they don't like about what they do.
- Go to career fairs
- Ask someone if you can shadow them on the job for a few days.
- Participate in an internship
- Participate in work-based learning
- Volunteer
- Take CTE classes
- Go on field trips

Luckily, there are many good resources available for career exploration. Some schools have a career center. If this is the case for you, then that would be a great place to start. Also, some local libraries have career systems in place. If not, though, do not despair because there are other options.

The Internet is full of reliable websites that help you learn about careers and career exploration. Don't be afraid to explore sites designed by specific states even if you live elsewhere. Often, a majority of the information will be pertinent regardless of where you live.

Here are some good free tests that can help guide you towards careers based on your interests and skills:

Occupational Outlook Handbook: This online handbook allows you to look at jobs based on groups, areas, growth, education, and pay. For each job, you can see what they do, the work environment, the education needed, the pay, the job outlook, and similar occupations. http://www.bls.gov/ooh/

Holland Code Career Test: Helps you identify career interest among six themes: realistic, investigative, artistic, social, enterprising, and conventional. Offers a list of suggested careers based on the profile. http://www.truity.com/test/holland-code-career-test

Here are other sites that can guide you through the entire career maze:

California Career Café: Created for community college students, this site is free and useful to high school students as well. It helps you identify your strengths, talents, interests and educational options. It also helps you explore careers, connects you to employers, and teaches you what soft skills are needed by these employers. http://www.cacareercafe.com/

California Career Zone: A career exploration and planning system designed for students. This site has information on over 900 occupations. It has many profiler tests, as well as career videos, and job openings. https://www.cacareerzone.org

Engineergirl.org: This site is for girls interested in learning more about engineering opportunities. www.engeineergirl.org.

O'Net Online: At O'Net, you can enter a work or title, look up careers by expected job growth, by career cluster, by green economy sector, by industry, by job family, by STEM discipline, and by education, experience, and training necessary. As jobs are located, O'Net provides information about the tasks, tools, technology, knowledge, skills, abilities, work activities, work context, job zone, education, credentials, interests, work styles, work values, related occupations, wages, employment, and job openings. https://www.onetonline.org/

The point to this exploration is to help you career possibilities of interest. During this stage, your career interests will grow, develop, and change. That is great! The more information you have, the better able you will be to make a final decision that meets your needs.

Step 3: Set a Tentative Career Goal

After you have spent time researching yourself and potential careers, it is time to pick a tentative career goal. Keep in mind that this goal is for a first career and it is only tentative. You are not picking what you will do for the rest of your life. You are simply deciding on your first job. If, after more exploration, you want to make a change, it will be much easier because you've already done the first three steps.

Remember, you need to set a career goal that is based on your interests plus your personality and abilities. You need to make a Plan A and a back-up Plan B so you are prepared to pivot in response to life's many uncertainties, such as the changing job market and emerging career opportunities. This is especially true if you are entrepreneurial. 63% of those in their twenties want to be their own boss...and creating good jobs while rebuilding America's middle-class hinges on the success of small businesses and startups.[12]

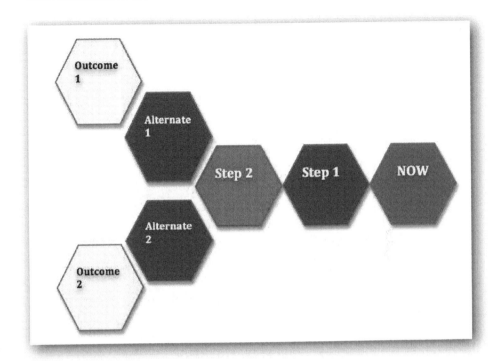

Step 4: Create a Skill-Based Education Plan

The fourth step is to create a Skill-Based Education Plan to prepare for what you will do after school. This plan should include your tentative career goal, the skills and knowledge you will need to gain, and the realistic steps (education, training, experiences) you plan to take to get there. Having such a plan will help you when you pursue an internship, select a college major, and seek employment. Also, be sure to make both a Plan A and a Plan B. Setbacks are inevitable; but don't worry! It's how you respond to these challenges that matters. I suggest developing strong coping skills and learning how to work well in teams. It is important to be able to pivot quickly and persevere down an alternative path towards your goal when obstacles arise.

Making a plan is going to require some out of the box thinking. Don't get stuck in the "4-year college for everyone" rut. There are many options available, many of which do not require a 4-year degree. Some of these include:

1. Career and Technical Education (CTE)
2. Bachelor's Degree
3. Bachelor's Degree in Technology
4. 2-year Associates Degree
5. 1-year technical certificates
6. Regional Occupation Program (ROP)
7. Military Service
8. Online Education
9. A year studying abroad
10. A prep/gap year
11. Private Career Schools and Colleges
12. Full-time Employment
13. Formal Apprenticeships/Internships
14. Religious Missionary Service
15. Peace Corps or other International Volunteer Program
16. Americorps or other National Service Program
17. Volunteer Work
18. Adult Schools

For instance, if you want to be an interior designer, you will find that there are certificate programs, 2-year associate programs, and 4-year programs available. When it comes to certifications, there are core, advanced, and specialty courses available. Additionally, you may want to think about an internship or apprenticeship.[13] You will consider your interest in more schooling, the cost of schooling, the location of training, the amount of money you will make with additional training, the ability to get training while working, along with many other factors.

Finally, while in high school, you may want to consider getting a job that uses interior design skills such as merchandise display, wallpaper hanger, or painter. If you can't find work with an interior designer, you could look for work in similar fields such as architecture or floral design. You will also want to consider high school classes that give you the types of skills needed to be an interior designer such as a communications class that will teach you to convey oral information effectively, classes that help you with critical thinking, and geometry classes that teach you how to calculate the amount of paint or wallpaper you need to order.

This plan will be the blueprint for what classes you take in high school, the post-secondary programs you wish to complete, and the institutions you apply to attend. Because of this plan, you will see the reason behind the courses you take and find true relevance to your coursework. Two of the best ways to create a Skills-Based Education Plan are:

1. DreamCatcher: Identify your purpose in life and achieve your career dreams through eight interactive lessons. Each lesson is interactive with great videos and an online tool to talk to other students with similar career interests. www.TelosES.com

2. California Career Center: This is a career planning website to help you create an education plan with many different options. It will also help you develop career self-management skills. https://www.calcareercenter.org/

Ultimately, your first career choice is a personal decision, and it may change many times. The best thing you can do is to gain technical skills, academic knowledge, and employability skills. The work ethic and academic knowledge you are acquiring by challenging yourself in high school will serve you well as you pursue your next steps in life.

Identifying those careers which align to who you are will ensure that you are happy and financially secure because of your skilled, competitive advantage. That is how you align a pattern for yourself for a successful career. Remember to always be true to who you are, strive to fulfill your full potential, and bring passion to whatever you do.

---

1 Epperson, S. (August 28, 2012). No College Degree Required for these $100,000 jobs. *USA Today*. And: Godofsky, J., Zukin, C., & Van Horn, C. (2011). *Unfulfilled Expectations: Recent College Graduates Struggle in a Troubled Economy.* John J. Heldrich Center for Workforce Development, Rutgers. And: Jacobson, L., et al. (2009). *Pathways to Boosting the Earnings of Low-Income students by Increasing their Educational Attainment,* Gates Foundation/Hudson Institute.

2 United States; US Census Bureau; 2014, http://www.statista.com/statistics/233301/median-household-income-in-the-united-states-by-education/

3 California Labor Market Information Division, Employment Development Department data.

4 California Labor Market Information Division, Employment Development Department data, 10 and 90 percentile excluding sole proprietorships.

5 Remarks of President Barack Obama – Address to Joint Session of Congress. Tuesday, February 24th, 2009. https://www.whitehouse.gov/the-press-office/remarks-president-barack-obama-address-joint-session-congress

6 Gray, K. & Herr, E. (2006). *Other Ways to Win: Creating Alternatives for High School Graduates. Third Edition.* Thousand Oaks: Corwin Press.

7 U.S. Census Bureau, 2012, Table PINC-03; U.S. Census Bureau, 2012a

8 http://futureworkplace.com/wp-content/uploads/MultipleGenAtWork_infographic.pdf

9 "Bureau of Labor Statistics, U.S. Department of Labor, 2014–2015 Occupational Outlook Handbook, [date accessed] [http://www.bls.gov/ooh/]."

10 https://www.onetonline.org/find/career?c=0&g=Go

11 Michigan State University. "Parents still major influence on child's decision to pursue science careers." ScienceDaily. ScienceDaily, 21 February 2010. <www.sciencedaily.com/releases/2010/02/100220204814.htm>.

12 http://www.phoenix.edu/news/releases/2015/08/uopx_workplace_survey_finds_more_than_one_third_working_adults_consider_themselves_intrapreneurs.html

13 http://www.onetonline.org/link/summary/27-1025.00

APPENDIX C

INCOME RANKING QUESTIONNAIRE

(for California's Labor Market)

Rank these 10 occupations in order of their hourly wage/earnings. Leave the Hourly Wage and Education columns blank. (Highest income = #1. Lowest income = #10)

Ranking	Hourly Wage	Education
_____Air Traffic Controllers	_____	_____
_____Dental Hygienists	_____	_____
_____Electrical Power-Line Installers/Repairers	_____	_____
_____Diagnostic medical sonographers	_____	_____
_____Elevator installers & repairers	_____	_____
_____Geographer	_____	_____
_____Market Research Analysts	_____	_____
_____Writers and Authors	_____	_____
_____Community & Social Service Specialists	_____	_____
_____Mental Health Counselors	_____	_____

Rank these 10 occupations in order of their hourly wage/earnings. Leave the Hourly Wage and Education columns blank. (Highest income = #1. Lowest income = #10)

Ranking	Hourly Wage	Education
_____First-Line Supervisors of Police/Detectives	_____	_____
_____Radiation Therapists	_____	_____
_____Power Distributors & Dispatchers	_____	_____
_____Logistics & Distribution Managers	_____	_____
_____Computer Network Support Specialists	_____	_____
_____Soil and Plant Scientists	_____	_____
_____Anthropologists & Archeologists	_____	_____
_____Athletic Trainers	_____	_____
_____Music Directors & Composers	_____	_____
_____Radio & Television Announcers	_____	_____

APPENDIX D

INCOME RANKING QUESTIONNAIRE ANSWERS

(for California's Labor Market)

Rank these 10 occupations in order of their hourly wage/earnings. Leave the Hourly Wage and Education columns blank. (Highest income = #1. Lowest income = #10)

Ranking		Hourly Wage	Education
1	Air Traffic Controllers	$62.90	Associates
2	Dental Hygienists	$48.02	Associates
3	Electrical Power-Line Installers/Repairers	$46.19	Apprenticeship/OJT
4	Diagnostic Medical Sonographers	$41.46	Associates
5	Elevator Installers and Repairers	$40.62	CTE cert / OJT
6	Geographer	$36.65	Bachelors
7	Market Research Analysts	$33.01	Bachelors
8	Writers and Authors	$24.80	Bachelors
9	Community & Social Service Specialists	$22.73	Master's Degree
10	Mental Health Counselors	$19.43	Master's Degree

Rank these 10 occupations in order of their hourly wage/earnings. Leave the Hourly Wage and Education columns blank. (Highest income = #1. Lowest income = #10)

Ranking		Hourly Wage	Education
1	First-Line Supervisors of Police/Detectives	$60.91	CTE cert / OJT
2	Radiation Therapists	$46.65	Associates
3	Power Distributors & Dispatchers	$42.92	CTE cert / OJT
4	Logistics & Distribution Managers	$40.63	Associates
5	Computer Network Support Specialists	$35.14	Associates
6	Soil and Plant Scientists	$31.21	Bachelors
7	Anthropologists & Archeologists	$27.34	Master's Degree
8	Athletic Trainers	$23.73	Bachelors
9	Music Directors & Composers	$23.11	Bachelors
10	Radio & Television Announcers	$17.29	Bachelors

Data Source: EMSI occupation employment data based on Occupational Employment Statistics (QCEW and Non-QCEW Employees classes of worker) and the American Community Survey (Self-Employed and Extended Proprietors).

APPENDIX E

ADDITIONAL RESOURCES

Here are some additional resources, many of which are free. They are each a great place start for teachers, parents, and students alike.

Self-Exploration

O'Net Online Skills Search: This allows students to choose skills from six different skill groups including basic skills, complex problem-solving skills, resource management skills, social skills, systems skills, and technical skills.

https://www.onetonline.org/skills/

Career InfoNet Skills Profiler: This allows students to choose from seven different skill groups including basic skills, social skills, complex problem-solving skills, technical skills, system skills, resource management skills, and desktop computer skills.

http://www.careerinfonet.org/skills/skills_list.aspx

ISeek Skills Assessment: Lets your students rate themselves on 35 skills and see which occupations match those skills.

http://www.iseek.org/careers/skillsAssessment

Career Values Scale: These 88 questions look at your student's values and see how they relate to work. This will help your student determine the level of satisfaction they will derive from different careers.

http://quintcareers.testingroom.com/

Work Preference Inventory: Twenty-four questions will assess your student's work style.

http://www.careerperfect.com/services/free/work-preference/

Personality Assessments

CA CareerZone Interest Profiler: Occupational interests are identified through a series of questions about work activities that some people do on their jobs. Based on the aforementioned Holland Code, it includes comprehensive information on over 900 occupations.

https://www.cacareerzone.org/ip/

Jung Typology Test: Helps identify one's lifestyle preferences, personality strengths, and suitably aligned career choices.

http://www.humanmetrics.com/

Myers-Briggs Type Indicator (MBTI): This personality test builds upon Jung's typologies and is one of the most reliable and trusted. It has been selected by the nation's top colleges to help with career development and is backed by scientific research.[1] This test will help your students understand themselves and how they interact with others. It will help them identify their preferences in four areas: where they focus their attention, how they take in information, how they make decisions based on the information, and how they deal with the world. The original test costs $49.95, however, a free version can be found at:

http://www.truity.com/test/type-finder-research-edition.

Keirsey Temperament Sorter (KTS-II): This test is similar to the MBTI. However, it breaks up the MBTI's 16 types into 4 basic categories: Artisans, Guardians, Rationals, and Idealists.

http://www.keirsey.com/sorter/register.aspx

Inner Heroes: This test is a combination of the MBTI and the KTS-II.
http://www.innerheroes.com/quiz.asp

Personality Index: This examines personality features that influence how your student approaches work, interactions, and activities.

http://quintcareers.testingroom.com/

Big Five Personality Test: Once called All About You, this tests measures personality as it applies to careers.

http://www.outofservice.com/bigfive/

DiSC: Helps your student learn how they respond to conflict, their motivations, their stressors, and how they solve problems.

http://discpersonalitytesting.com/free-disc-test/

ColorCode: Identifies driving core motives, helping students understand why they do what they do.

https://www.colorcode.com/free_personality_test/

Career Exploration

Career Interest Profiler: 180-question assessment measures occupation and career interests.

http://quintcareers.testingroom.com/

Career Interest Test: 100-question assessment identifies career interests and suggests specific jobs related to those interests.

http://www.livecareer.com/career-test

Occupational Outlook Handbook: This online handbook allows students to look at jobs based on groups, areas, growth, education, and pay. For each job, the student can see what they do, the work environment, the education needed, the pay, the job outlook, and similar occupations.

http://www.bls.gov/ooh/

Holland Code Career Test: Helps students identify career interest among six themes: realistic, investigative, artistic, social, enterprising, and conventional. Offers a list of suggested careers based on the profile.

http://www.truity.com/test/holland-code-career-test

ASVAB - Multiple-choice test that helps a student identify which Army jobs are best for them. The entire test is done through a military recruiting office, but sample tests can be found online.

https://www.4tests.com/asvab

California Career Café: Created for community college students, this site is free and useful to high school students as well. It helps them identify their strengths, talents, interests and educational options. It also helps students explore careers, connect them to employers, and teach them what soft skills are needed by these employers.

http://www.cacareercafe.com/

California Career Zone: A career exploration and planning system designed for students. This site has information on over 900 occupations. It has many profiler tests, as well as career videos, and job openings.
https://www.cacareerzone.org

California Career Center: This is a career planning website helping students find an education plan with many different options. It will help your students develop career self-management skills.
https://www.calcareercenter.org/

Engineergirl.org: This site is for girls interested in learning more about engineering opportunities.
www.engeineergirl.org.

Road Trip Nation: Stories told by people in a myriad of occupations help create the resources that will show your students the many different careers and possibilities available.
http://roadtripnation.com

Dirty Jobs: A Discovery Channel series with Mike Rowe. He assumes the duties of the job he profiles for the week, helping students gain an appreciation for the many different jobs available and what makes people happy in those jobs other consider "too dirty."
http://www.discovery.com/tv-shows/dirty-jobs/

Whodouwant2b.com: Though focused on California, this is a good site to help students determine courses to take and career options.
http://whodouwant2b.com/student/pathways

Jobs Made Real: Website designed to aid teens in discovering their career path. Features videos of people during their jobs. Also provides statistical data on job forecast and career information.
http://www.jobsmadereal.com/

The Support Personnel Accountability Report Card: The SPARC online tool enables school site student support teams to create a unique, publishable document highlighting the impact their staff and programs are having on student career and college readiness.
www.sparconline.net

O'Net Online: At O'Net, a student can enter a work or title, look up careers by expected job growth, by career cluster, by green economy sector, by industry, by job family, by STEM discipline, and by education, experience, and training necessary. As jobs are located, O'Net provides information about the tasks, tools, technology, knowledge, skills, abilities, work activities, work context, job zone, education, credentials, interests, work styles, work values, related occupations, wages, employment, and job openings.

https://www.onetonline.org/

Real Talk Career App: Provides relevant and timely advice from over 400 young professionals of varying careers. Information on education and breaking into the career.

https://play.google.com/store/apps/details?id=com.learningpartnership.realtalk

Gingiks YouTube Channel: Videos of people with interesting jobs all shot by high school students.

https://www.youtube.com/channel/UCgS_1_CtAfdr2JJtKI6vi8w

Career One Stop: US. Department of Labor website with career exploration tools, occupational videos, labor market and wage data, and job searching resources.

http://www.careeronestop.org/

Career Surfer: This mobile application is a tool for beginning career exploration and planning. Students can explore careers on their mobile devices by viewing snapshots of the more than 900 occupations detailed on the California CareerZone. Career Surfer is a free download from the Apple App Store or Google Play.

---

1 https://www.cpp.com/products/mbti/index.aspx

36916621R00125

Made in the USA
San Bernardino, CA
05 August 2016